Watch Out for Wolves

*Keys to Discerning Authentic Ministries
and Evaluating Doctrinal Trends*

Bill Scheidler

Watch Out for Wolves
© Copyright 2022 by Bill Scheidler
All Rights Reserved

Printed by BT Johnson Publishing
www.BTJohnsonPublishing.com

Other Translations Used:

Gdspd – The New Testament: An American Translation / by Edgar J. Goodspeed. Chicago, Ill.: University of Chicago Press, 1923. Used by permission. All Rights Reserved.

NEB – The New English Bible. Copyright © 1970 by Cambridge University Press. Used by permission. All Rights Reserved.

NIV – The Holy Bible, New International Version. Copyright © 1973, 1978, 1984, by International Bible Society. Used by permission of Zondervan Publishing House. All Rights Reserved.

Rieu – The Four Gospels / a new translation from the Greek by E.V. Rieu. Baltimore: Penguin Books, 1953. Used by permission. All Rights Reserved.

TCNT – The Twentieth Century New Testament. Copyright © 1904 by Fleming H. Revell Company. Used by permission. All Rights Reserved.

Printed in the United States
ALL RIGHTS RESERVED
ISBN: 978-1-952645-34-1

Contents

Part 1 – Discerning Authentic Ministries

Forward..5

1 – The Need for Spiritual Discernment..................9-21

2 – The Fact of False Ministries............................23-40

   Appendix: The Context of the Last Days..............41-42

3 – The Food and Fuel of False Ministries............43-58

4 – The Face, Fruit and Fate of False Ministries...59-73

5 – Keeping Ourselves Pure....................................75-83

   Appendix: Judging Prophecy...............................84-97

Part 2 – Discerning Doctrinal Trends

6 – Defining "Current Trends"...........................101-108

7 – The Challenge of Relevancy.........................109-117

8 – The Challenge of Balance.............................119-130

9 – The Challenge of Discerning the Winds.......133-159

10 – Present Day Trends.....................................161-170

Forward

We are living in very interesting times. They are interesting because current events seem to be moving us very quickly into times and seasons in God's economy that are consistent with end-time events. I know what you are saying, "We have heard this before." Yes, that is true.

You will notice that I did not say that we are in the end times. However, I will say that many of the things indicated by the prophets of the Old and New Testament and warnings given to us by Jesus Himself, seem to be particularly applicable to and relevant in our world today.

The Church of Jesus Christ has always had its challenges. Jesus warned us that in the world we would have tribulation, we would most likely be persecuted and we would suffer for being identified with Him. Even though this is a fact, it has never been something that has stopped the Church or neutralized the Church from growing and from fulfilling its God-appointed mission.

The Church is built to withstand the forces of darkness that seek to undermine its effectiveness. The Church has proven that it can adapt to differing forms of government, oppressive regimes, and all-out assaults to destroy it. It has weathered them well by being flexible in its forms and responsive to the voice of the Holy Spirit.

The biggest danger for the Church has never been attacks from governments, other religious groups or atheistic zealots. The greatest danger has always been from forces working from within the Church. If Satan cannot weaken the Church from outside of the walls of the Church, he will infiltrate the Church and turn his attention to causing division, promoting heresy and destroying it from within.

To do this he will work in the hearts of influential people within the Church who can come under his influence and bring a tainted, good-sounding message that will have the potential of leading people astray. These ministries have the potential of neutralizing believers in their testimony, causing believers to focus on the wrong goal, and even causing them to stumble and fall.

Jesus warned us to watch out for deception (Mt. 24:24-25). He warned us that false ministries would arise teaching false doctrines that need to be discerned. My hope in this book is to reiterate Jesus' warning and to equip the believer to be able to discern the true from the false and the real from the counterfeit.

*Then we will no longer be immature like children. We won't be tossed and blown about by **every wind of new teaching**. We will not be influenced when people try to trick us with lies so clever they sound like the truth. Instead, we will speak the truth in love, growing in every way more and more like Christ, who is the head of His body, the church.* Ephesians 4:14-15

Part I

Discerning Authentic Ministries

Chapter 1
The Need for Discernment

The purpose of this book is to equip the believer to be able to distinguish the good from the bad, the wheat from the tares, the profitable from the unprofitable and the true from the counterfeit. The Bible speaks of deception and the need to be watchful especially as we near the Second Coming of Christ. As we approach that day, we must be able to discern or judge between true and false ministries and from sound and "not-so-sound" doctrine. We must be able to discern between ministries and doctrines that build what God is building and those ministries and doctrines that work against what God is building.

In order to be able to do this we need to:

- Observe the warnings of God's word,
- Accept the fact that we are all vulnerable to deception,
- Apply the tests that God gives to us in His word,
- Maintain a teachable heart and
- Lean strongly on the Holy Spirit to assist us.

Christianity is not a game, it is warfare. As Christians, we are called to be sober and vigilant in these days because we have an adversary who seeks to devour us. This adversary will use any and all means to thwart the purpose of God in our lives and in the life of the Church, the instrument of God's purpose in the earth. The biggest weapon or tool that he uses to do this is deception.

As believers we have to understand that there are times when the devil uses people and teachings, which are not obviously wicked, to lure us into deception. If the ability to distinguish between good and evil were easy, then there would be no possibility of deception. Often that which is damaging comes to us in "sheep's clothing." Therefore it is critical that we arm ourselves with the discernment or a skill in judging the true from the counterfeit.

> *And they shall teach My people the difference between the holy and the unholy and cause them to **discern between the unclean and the clean**.*
> Ezekiel 44:23

> *Then those who feared the LORD spoke to one another, and the LORD listened and heard them; so a book of remembrance was written before Him for those who fear the LORD and who meditate on His name. "They shall be Mine," says the LORD of hosts, "On the day that I make them My jewels. And I will spare them as a man spares his own son who serves him." Then you shall again **discern between the righteous and the wicked, between one who serves God and one who does not serve Him**.*
> Malachi 3:16-18

The Word "Discernment"

There are several definitions of "discern" that help us with our understanding. The English word "to discern" means some of the following:

1. To perceive with the eyes or intellect; to detect.
2. To recognize or comprehend mentally.
3. To perceive or recognize as being different or distinct; to distinguish.

4. To perceive differences.
5. To perceive and fix the identity of, especially with difficulty.
6. To perceive, especially barely or fleetingly.
7. To perceive with a special effort of the senses or the mind.
8. To recognize as being different.

Synonyms for the word "discern" include such words like perceive, observe, notice, note, recognize, tell apart and distinguish. To discern is the opposite of to disregard, neglect and overlook.

The definitions of the English word "discernment" can add even further to our understanding in this area. It means some of the following:

1. The act or process of exhibiting keen insight and good judgment.
2. Keenness of insight and judgment.
3. Skill in perceiving, discriminating, or judging.

Synonyms include: acumen, astuteness, clear-sightedness, discrimination, eye, keenness, nose, perceptiveness and shrewdness. It is the opposite of gullibility, denseness, ignorance, ineptness, obtuseness and stupidity

The Greek words that are most often translated "discern" or discernment" are *diakrisis* and *dokimazo*. *Diakrisis* means distinguishing, discerning or judging. It is used by the writer to the Hebrews in Hebrews 5:14.

*But solid food belongs to those who are of full age, that is, those who by reason of use have their **senses exercised to discern both good and evil**.* Hebrews 5:14

The Bible indicates that the ability to discern is a mark of a mature believer. But many believers are not mature in this area and need to exercise their spiritual senses to discern. We are often good at exercising our physical body, but we need to be even better when it comes to exercising our spiritual senses.

The Greek word *dokimazo* literally means to test, examine, prove or scrutinize (to see whether a thing is genuine or not) as with metals. It is possible for something to look exactly like gold, but, in reality, it is fool's gold. If you take what you perceive to be a gold ring into a pawn shop for cash, the first thing they will do is test it for gold content. It may be pure gold, it may be a mixture of gold with another metal, or it may not contain any gold at all. This is what we are to do with ministries and doctrines. Jesus fully expects us to be able use discernment in a spiritual way, not simply a natural way.

*Hypocrites! You can **discern** the face of the sky and of the earth, but how is it you do not **discern** this time?*
Luke 12:56

*Beloved, do not believe every spirit, but **test the spirits**, whether they are of God; because many false prophets have gone out into the world.* 1 John 4:1

Test all things; *hold fast what is good.*
1 Thessalonians 5:21

On the other hand, don't be gullible. Check out everything, and keep only what's good. –Msg

Discernment Needed Today

If ever there was a time that we needed discernment, it is now. The devil would like nothing more than to pollute the Church. The closer we get to the return of Christ the more he is in panic mode. He knows that his days are numbered and he is throwing everything he has at the Church.

The devil is subtle and uses deception as his main tool (Gen. 3:1; 2 Cor. 11:3). This is why Paul was so concerned about the believers in Corinth.

But I fear, lest somehow, as the serpent deceived Eve by his craftiness, so your minds may be corrupted from the simplicity that is in Christ. 2 Corinthians 11:3

Christianity is basically simple. It is the devil who tries to complicate it by his subtlety. His primary task is to deceive and his primary weapon is deception. To deceive is to cause to stray, to lead astray, lead aside from the right way through craft or trickery. The devil is an expert at deception. The Bible repeatedly warns us against the "wiles of the devil" (Eph. 6:11).

*Put on the whole armor of God, that you may be able to stand against the **wiles of the devil**.* Ephesians 6:11

The Greek word used in the above passage for "wiles" refers to cunning arts, deceit, craft and trickery. Peter warned us in his first epistle that the devil is seeking whom he may devour (1 Pet. 5:8-9).

*Be sober, be vigilant; because your adversary the devil walks about like a roaring lion, **seeking whom he may devour**. Resist him, steadfast in the faith, knowing that the same sufferings are experienced by your brotherhood in the world.*

Paul told his son in the faith to help people escape the trap or snares of the devil (2 Tim. 2:23-26).

*Gently instruct those who oppose the truth. Perhaps God will change those people's hearts, and they will learn the truth. Then they will come to their senses and escape from **the devil's trap**. For they have been held captive by him to do whatever he wants.*
2 Timothy 2:25-26, NLT

A snare is an instrument for hunting. It is a trap that is set for something or someone that is hidden from obvious view. When a snare seizes its prey it is usually unexpected, sudden and without warning.

Paul further warns us that at times the devil will use people in ministry to trick or deceive believers (Eph. 4:14).

Then we will no longer be immature like children. We won't be tossed and blown about by every wind of new teaching. We will not be influenced **when people try to trick us with lies so clever they sound like the truth**. Ephesians 4:14, NLT

God wants His people to be as wise as serpents (Mt. 10:16). Sometimes the wolves about which we are warned are not just the unsaved who bring persecution to the church, sometimes the wolves actually arise from within the church and damage the work of God (Acts 20:29-30).

For I know this, that after my departure savage wolves will come in among you, not sparing the flock. ***Also from among yourselves*** *men will rise up, speaking perverse things, to draw away the disciples after themselves.* Acts 20:29-30

The Book of Proverbs offers these cautions:

The simple believes every word, but the prudent considers well his steps. Proverbs 14:15

A prudent man foresees evil and hides himself, but the simple pass on and are punished. Proverbs 22:3

A prudent person foresees danger and takes precautions. The simpleton goes blindly on and suffers the consequences. Proverbs 22:3, NLT

This message is very important for us today as we draw closer to Christ's return. Jesus said that the last days will be especially characterized by a prevalence of deception (Mt. 24:4, 24; Mark 13:5; Luke 21:8). When referencing the context of His return He said,

*"Take heed that no one **deceives** you. For many will come in My name, saying, 'I am the Christ,' and will **deceive many**."* Matthew 24:4b-5

Jesus made it clear that there will be many false and deceptive ministries or false anointed ones (Mt. 24:5; Mark 13:6, 21-23).

*Then if anyone says to you, "Look, here is the Christ!" or, "Look, He is there!" do not believe it. For false christs and false prophets will rise and show signs and wonders to **deceive**, if possible, even the elect. But take heed; see, I have told you all things beforehand.* Mark 13:21-23

*"Then if anyone tells you, 'Look, here is the Messiah,' or 'There he is,' don't believe it. For false messiahs and false prophets will rise up and perform signs and wonders so as to **deceive**, if possible, even God's chosen ones. Watch out! I have warned you about this ahead of time!* Mark 13:21-13, NLT

In addition, there will be many deceptive signs and wonders (Mt. 24:24; Mark 13:22; 2 Th. 2:9).

*For false Christ's and false prophets will rise and show great signs and wonders to **deceive**, if possible, even the elect.* Matthew 24:24

Other New Testament writers confirm that the end times will be times of great deception. There will be many false and deceptive doctrines (1 Tim. 4:1).

> *Now the Spirit expressly says that in latter times some will depart from the faith, giving heed to **deceiving spirits** and doctrines of demons...* 1 Timothy 4:1

Because of the prevalence of false ministries espousing false doctrines, the end time context will sift out those who have a love for the truth and those who do not (2 Th. 2:8-12).

> *And then the lawless one will be revealed, whom the Lord will consume with the breath of His mouth and destroy with the brightness of His coming. 9 The coming of the lawless one is according to the working of Satan, with all power, signs, and lying wonders, 10 and with all unrighteous **deception** among those who perish, because they did not receive the love of the truth, that they might be saved. 11 And for this reason God will send them **strong delusion**, that they should believe the lie, 12 that they all may be condemned who did not believe the truth but had pleasure in unrighteousness.* 2 Thessalonians 2:8-12

This end time context will be characterized by some being deluded and departing from the faith (1 Tim. 4:1).

> *Now the Spirit expressly says that in latter times some will depart from the faith, giving heed to deceiving spirits and doctrines of demons, speaking lies in hypocrisy, having their own conscience seared with a hot iron...* 1 Timothy 4:1

This end time context will see church-goers open to deception through selfishness and covetousness (2 Tim. 3:1-9, 13).

> *But know this, that in the last days perilous times will come: 2 For men will be lovers of themselves, lovers of money, boasters, proud, blasphemers, disobedient to parents, unthankful, unholy, 3 unloving, unforgiving, slanderers, without self-control, brutal, despisers of good, 4 traitors, headstrong, haughty, lovers of*

*pleasure rather than lovers of God, 5 having a form of godliness but denying its power. And from such people turn away! 6 For of this sort are those who creep into households and make captives of gullible women loaded down with sins, led away by various lusts, 7 always learning and never able to come to the knowledge of the truth. 8 Now as Jannes and Jambres resisted Moses, so do these also resist the truth: men of corrupt minds, disapproved concerning the faith; 9 but they will progress no further, for their folly will be manifest to all, as theirs also was....**But evil men and impostors will grow worse and worse, deceiving and being deceived.***
2 Timothy 3:1-9, 13

This end time context will see people itching for the strange and the unusual (2 Tim. 4:3-4). Or could we say the spectacular.

For the time will come when they will not endure sound doctrine, but according to their own desires, because they have itching ears, they will heap up for themselves teachers; and they will turn their ears away from the truth and be turned aside to fables.
2 Timothy 4:3-4

It is not usually the basic foods properly prepared that cause you grief. It is more often the exotic things that become dangerous.

This end time context will witness the devil unleashing his full fury on the Church (Rev. 12:9; 13:14). Satan knows a lot about the declared words of God. He knows that if God's word is true, his days are numbered and the closer we get to Christ's return, the closer he is to his complete demise. He is like a rat trapped in a corner that is now becoming violent and lashing out at anything and everything to try to preserve whatever life it has left.

Areas to be Discerned

I think we have established the fact that the closer we get to the return of the Lord, the harder the devil is going to work to lead us into deception. It is obvious that as Christians, we need discernment in several areas. As we move forward in this book, we will be focusing on discerning three main areas that must be discerned.

The first area that requires discernment is in relation to the **ministries** from which we are feeding.

> *Now I urge you, brethren, note those who cause divisions and offenses, contrary to the doctrine which you learned, and avoid them. For those who are such do not serve our Lord Jesus Christ, but their own belly, and* ***by smooth words and flattering speech deceive the hearts of the simple****. For your obedience has become known to all. Therefore I am glad on your behalf; but I want you to be wise in what is good, and simple concerning evil.*
> *Romans 16:17-19*

> *I appeal to you, brethren, to be on your guard concerning those who create dissensions and difficulties and cause divisions, in opposition to the doctrine (the teaching) which you have been taught. [I warn you to turn aside from them, to] avoid them. For such persons do not serve our Lord Christ but their own appetites and base desires, and by ingratiating and flattering speech, they beguile the hearts of the unsuspecting and simpleminded [people]. For while your loyalty and obedience is known to all, so that I rejoice over you, I would have you well versed and wise as to what is good and innocent and guileless as to what is evil.* –Amp

> *And now I make one more appeal, my dear brothers and sisters. Watch out for people who cause divisions and upset people's faith by teaching things that are*

contrary to what you have been taught. Stay away from them. Such people are not serving Christ our Lord; they are serving their own personal interests. By smooth talk and glowing words they deceive innocent people. But everyone knows that you are obedient to the Lord. This makes me very happy. I want you to see clearly what is right and to stay innocent of any wrong. –NLT

We do not want to become critical and judgmental, but we do not want to be gullible either. The truth is that many false ministers or ministries that can lead us into deception look almost exactly like the true.

The five-fold ministry was given to the church to equip the saints for works of service and to build up the Body of Christ (Eph. 4:11-12. Everything that these ministries do is for the sake of Christ and others.

However, as we will see in the next chapter, there are ministries who take advantage of the ministry anointing that they have for their own purposes and actually misrepresent Christ and abuse the people of God. Just as there are true apostles, prophets, evangelists, pastors and teachers, there are false apostles, prophets, evangelist, pastors and teachers. It is the responsibility of mature believers to be watchful and prepared at times to render judgment.

The second area that requires discernment is in relation to **doctrine or teachings** that we embrace (Eph. 4:11-16).

*And He Himself gave some to be apostles, some prophets, some evangelists, and some pastors and teachers, 12 for the equipping of the saints for the work of ministry, for the edifying of the body of Christ, 13 till we all come to the unity of the faith and of the knowledge of the Son of God, to a perfect man, to the measure of the stature of the fullness of Christ; 14 that we should no longer be children, tossed to and fro and carried about with **every wind of doctrine**,* *by the trickery of men, in the cunning craftiness of deceitful plotting, 15 but, speaking the truth in love, may grow up in all things into Him who is the head--Christ--16 from whom the whole body, joined and knit together by what every joint supplies, according to the effective working by which every part does its share, causes growth of the body for the edifying of itself in love.* Ephesians 4:11-16

We do not want to be those who believe or accept every wind of doctrine that is preached in our day, even if that teaching comes through those we consider to be reputable. We want to be discriminating like the Berean believers who searched the Scriptures to see if these things were true (Acts 17:11).

Then the brethren immediately sent Paul and Silas away by night to Berea. When they arrived, they went into the synagogue of the Jews. These were more fair-minded than those in Thessalonica, in that they received the word with all readiness, and searched the Scriptures daily to find out whether these things were so. Acts 17:10-11

It is not a sign of rebellion to challenge what is being said by leaders in the church or to question things that are written in Christian literature or on Christian websites. In fact, Paul had good things to say about these Berean believers who were open to new understanding, but before they bought in 100 percent, they were going to check it all out.

The NIV says this about the Berean believers:

*Now the Bereans **were of more noble character** than the Thessalonians, for they received the message with great eagerness and examined the Scriptures every day to see if what Paul said was true.*—NIV

A leader never has to be afraid of listeners who search the scripture to see if the things that they are teaching are truly scriptural. People who do so are not "rebels," they are, as Luke says, "of more noble character."

There are different reactions that we can have to new truth.

1. We can reject immediately without even giving it a fair hearing. This is skepticism and it is folly (Pro. 18:13).

2. We can accept it immediately without any examination of or testing of the truth. This is dangerous. We are to test all things (1 Th. 5:21). This is gullibility.

3. We can be like the Bereans. We can receive it with a good spirit and search it out to discover if it is true. This is wisdom.

The third area that requires discernment is in relation to **our own hearts** (Ps. 139:23-24). We are all weak and vulnerable as believers. The more we acknowledge our own vulnerability the more we can keep from being personally deceived. The more we realize how much we need the Lord the more success that we will have.

As we study this area in the pages ahead, we have to open our own hearts up to the Lord and allow Him to examine us and remove any of the things that might lead us to be those who could be labeled false. At the same time, we need to examine our hearts to see if there is anything in us or our thought processes that makes us particularly vulnerable to the deceptive teaching or practices of ministries that might be labeled false.

Search me, O God, and know my heart; try me, and know my anxieties; and see if there is any wicked way in me and lead me in the way everlasting.
Psalm 130:23

Chapter 2
The Fact of False Ministries

If you only read the Bible casually, you do not realize how often it warns us about false teachings and false teachers or ministries. When we do read about them we often presume that what is being said is not particularly relevant to us, because we would never be duped by such things. The reality is that every believer needs to be on guard. We live in day when a certain amount of skepticism can serve us well.

I am sure, like me, that you receive email, text messages or some other form of communication from time to time that seems too good to be true. When I get an email that tells me "I am a winner" in a contest that I did not enter, I have my doubts. Or when I get a negative message that indicates that my accounts will be shut down if I do not respond immediately to their warning and call 1-800-YOU-DUPE, I am a little suspicious. I have had many phone calls about my warranty expiring on my 25-year-old car.

Before I had any tech savvy, I would be tempted to respond to some of these (I said "tempted"). As time has gone on and I have educated myself regarding scams, click bait and other hustles, I have learned how to red flag, delete and report them without responding.

I would not have lasted very long in the current tech world, if I had just blindly trusted everything that I received or read from these messages. The same is true when it comes to our spiritual life. We need to accept the reality that everything is not as it appears. If we ignore the problem, if we fall for the deception, it could end up being very costly.

The End Time Church in Context

The Bible reveals that the last days will see some very positive things happening and at the same time some very negative things happening.

Let's start by looking at some of the positive things that we can expect prior to the return of the Lord. On the **positive side**, we can expect that the Eternal Purpose of God or God's plan of the ages will come to completion (Is. 60:1-5).

> *Arise, shine; for your light has come! And the glory of the LORD is risen upon you. 2 For behold, the darkness shall cover the earth, and deep darkness the people; but the LORD will arise over you, and His glory will be seen upon you. 3 The Gentiles shall come to your light, and kings to the brightness of your rising. 4 Lift up your eyes all around, and see: they all gather together, they come to you; your sons shall come from afar, and your daughters shall be nursed at your side. 5 Then you shall see and become radiant, and your heart shall swell with joy; because the abundance of the sea shall be turned to you, the wealth of the Gentiles shall come to you. Isaiah 60:1-5*

Some of the **positive things** that we can expect as we near this time include the following:

1. The church will be glorious and victorious (Mt. 16:18; Eph 5:27; Is. 60:13).

> *...that He might present her to Himself a glorious church, not having spot or wrinkle or any such thing, but that she should be holy and without blemish. Ephesians 5:27*

2. There will be days of great harvest which means a great ingathering of souls the likes of which the world has never seen (Mt. 13:39; Rev. 14:14-16).

...the harvest is the end of the age... Matthew 13:39b
Then I looked, and behold, a white cloud, and on the cloud sat One like the Son of Man, having on His head a golden crown, and in His hand a sharp sickle. And another angel came out of the temple, crying with a loud voice to Him who sat on the cloud, "Thrust in Your sickle and reap, for the time has come for You to reap, for the harvest of the earth is ripe." So He who sat on the cloud thrust in His sickle on the earth, and the earth was reaped.
Revelation 14:14-16

3. There will be a great outpouring of the Spirit of God (Joel 2:28-32; Acts 2:17-18).

The prophecy of Joel was not fully fulfilled on the Day of Pentecost. When you read the words carefully from Joel's prophecy you realize that the language of Joel puts the context of this prophecy in the end times just prior to the Second Coming of Christ.

And it shall come to pass afterward that I will pour out My Spirit on all flesh; your sons and your daughters shall prophesy, your old men shall dream dreams, your young men shall see visions. 29 And also on My menservants and on My maidservants, I will pour out My Spirit in those days. 30 And I will show wonders in the heavens and in the earth: blood and fire and pillars of smoke. 31 The sun shall be turned into darkness, and the moon into blood, before the coming of the great and awesome day of the LORD. 32 And it shall come to pass that whoever calls on the name of the LORD shall be saved. Joel 2:28-32a

4. The spirit and power of Elijah will be on the Church bringing restoration to relationships (Mal. 4:5-6).

Behold, I will send you Elijah the prophet before the coming of the great and dreadful day of the LORD. And he will turn the hearts of the fathers to the children, and the hearts of the children to their fathers, lest I come and strike the earth with a curse.

5. The gospel will be going forth into the entire world (Mt. 24:14).

And this gospel of the kingdom will be preached in all the world as a witness to all the nations, and then the end will come.

6. The kingdom of God will come to full fruit, that is, the righteous will become more and more righteous (Jam. 5:7-8; Rev. 22:11, LB).

Therefore be patient, brethren, until the coming of the Lord. See how the farmer waits for the precious fruit of the earth, waiting patiently for it until it receives the early and latter rain. You also be patient. Establish your hearts, for the coming of the Lord is at hand. James 5:7-8

These are incredible things to look forward to as we near the coming of the Lord. But all is not positive. At the same time these positive things are happening, there will be some very negative things happening as well. On the **negative side**, Satan will work overtime to see that purpose thwarted. At the end of this chapter I have a chart that breaks down for us what the climate or context will be in the days preceding the coming of Christ (2 Tim. 3:1-5, See Appendix 1). Many of these things will be happening with "good" church-going people. The following are six things we can expect on the negative side:

1. The love of many will grow cold (Mt. 24:12).

And because lawlessness will abound, the love of many will grow cold.

2. There will be a great falling away (2 Th. 2:3).

   Let no one deceive you by any means; for that Day will not come unless the falling away comes first...

3. Many will give heed to seducing spirits and doctrines of devils (1 Tim. 4:1).

   Now the Spirit expressly says that in latter times some will depart from the faith, giving heed to deceiving spirits and doctrines of demons...

4. Many false Christ's or anointed ones will arise deceiving many (2 Tim. 3:13; Mt. 24:24).

   But evil men and impostors will grow worse and worse, deceiving and being deceived. 2 Timothy 3:13

5. Deception will be prevalent (Mt. 24:24).

   For false Christ's and false prophets will rise and show great signs and wonders to deceive, if possible, even the elect.

6. Wickedness will come to full fruit (Rom. 1:18-32; Rev. 22:11).

   "And when that time comes, all doing wrong will do it more and more; the vile will become more vile; good men will be better; those who are holy will continue on in greater holiness." Revelation 22:11, Living Bible

If this is indeed the context of the church of the last days, it is essential that believers be able to discern the true from the false. Believers must be equipped to tell the difference between true biblical ministries and false ministries. Equally, they must be able to know the difference between sound doctrine and doctrines of devils.

What is a false ministry?

The word false literally means contrary to the truth or fact. If you look up the word in a dictionary, the word "false" means "contrary to the truth or fact; deceptive; counterfeit; artificial; not real or genuine."

Perhaps the word counterfeit best helps us to understand this concept. In most of the currencies of the world, countries have done everything that they can to ensure against counterfeiting. There is a standard by which those currencies are judged based on the criteria of the creators.

Everything is taken into account in the making of money. There is special paper, special ink, particular chemicals, special combinations and gradations of the ink, unique serial numbers and proper signatures. In addition, most modern currencies have markers hidden within them so that even with the use of modern copying equipment they are almost impossible to duplicate.

God has a prescription for ministry and teaching that meets His standard as the manufacturer. Often we can be fooled by looking only on the surface. The false looks very much like the true. The difference often has to do with what is hidden on the inside.

> *Beware of false prophets, who come to you in sheep's clothing, but inwardly they are ravenous wolves.*
> Matthew 7:15

The FACT of False Ministries

The Bible teaches us clearly that false ministries are always mingled among the true. When Jesus delivered His parables of the kingdom in Matthew 13, He indicated that the wheat (sons of the kingdom) and tares (sons of the wicked one) are sown together and grow together (Mt. 13:24-30; 36-43).

> *Then Jesus sent the multitude away and went into the house. And His disciples came to Him, saying, "Explain to us the parable of the tares of the field." 37 He answered and said to them: "He who sows the good seed is the Son of Man. 38 The field is the world, the good seeds are the **sons of the kingdom**, but the tares are the **sons of the wicked one**. 39 The enemy who sowed them is the devil, the harvest is the end of the age, and the reapers are the angels. 40 Therefore as the tares are gathered and burned in the fire, so it will be at the end of this age. 41 The Son of Man will send out His angels, and they will gather out of His kingdom all things that offend, and those who practice lawlessness, 42 and will cast them into the furnace of fire. There will be wailing and gnashing of teeth. 43 Then the righteous will shine forth as the sun in the kingdom of their Father. He who has ears to hear, let him hear!"* Matthew 13:36-43

In this parable the seeds sown are people (in Matthew's first parable of the kingdom, the seed represents the word of God). Jesus spoke of two types of people that were sown in the same field. They looked so much alike that it was difficult to tell them apart until the time of harvest when they would be more and more manifest.

Jesus indicated that they would be fully manifest at the time of the harvest (Mt. 13:30). At harvest time, because tares (counterfeit wheat) are not filled with the heavy wheat corn, they stand straight up while the true wheat bows over from the weight of the kernel in its head. You could say that the one bowed over represents an act of humility before God.

> *Let both grow together until the harvest, and at the time of harvest I will say to the reapers, "First gather together the tares and bind them in bundles to burn them but gather the wheat into my barn."*
>   Matthew 13:30

False ministries were found in both the Old and the New Testament time. They had them in Old Testament times and God warned His people about prophets who prophesied falsely (Deut. 18:20-22). God even gave them tests to be able to distinguish between the true and the false.

> *But the prophet who presumes to speak a word in My name, which I have not commanded him to speak, or who speaks in the name of other gods, that prophet shall die. And if you say in your heart, "How shall we know the word which the LORD has not spoken?" -- when a prophet speaks in the name of the LORD, if the thing does not happen or come to pass, that is the thing which the LORD has not spoken; the prophet has spoken it presumptuously; you shall not be afraid of him.* Deuteronomy 18:20-22

In addition, there were false ministries in New Testament times (Rev. 2:2). Jesus addressed the Ephesian Church in the Book of Revelation.

> *I know your works, your labor, your patience, and that you cannot bear those who are evil. And you have tested those who say they are apostles and are not, and have found them liars...* Revelation 2:2

The Ephesian Church was especially vulnerable because it was located on a major highway to Rome. God commended the Ephesian Church for being willing to put apostles to the test rather than just accepting them at face value. Because the false is mingled with the true, it is necessary for them to be discerned (1 John 4:1-3).

In the Early Church they had to contend with three primary problems in this realm. First of all, here were people who had been converted from Judaism who did not fully understand the New Covenant who were attempting to entangle Christians again into the demands of the Mosaic Law. These people were referred to as Judaizers. The Book of Galatians was written by

Paul to address this wrong concept that was prevalent especially in many of the Gentile churches.

The second problem with which the Early Church had to contend were people who had overreacted to the message of grace and were turning liberty into license to sin (Rom. 6:1-2; Gal. 5:13). The book of 1 Corinthians deals with this issue in a local church where their tolerance for sin in their midst and casual attitude toward promiscuity was not productive in building a strong body of believers (1 Cor. 3:1-3; 5:1-5).

A third common problem faced by the Early Church were people who were professional beggars guised as prophets who moved from church to church preying on people's generosity until they wore out their welcome (2 Th. 3:10-12).

The *Didache* is one of the earliest Christian writings to have come down to us. It was written in the Second Century and was a church manual where many instructions regarding order in the church were given. The following is an excerpt from that document:

> *Now you should welcome anyone who comes your way and teaches you all we have been saying to you. But if the teacher proves himself a renegade and by teaching otherwise contradicts all this, pay no attention to him. But if his teaching furthers the Lord's righteousness and knowledge, welcome him as the Lord.*
>
> *Now about the apostles and prophets: Act in line with the gospel precept. Welcome every apostle on arriving, as if he were the Lord. But he must not stay beyond one day. In case of necessity, however, the next day too. If he stays three days, he is a false prophet. On departing, an apostle must not accept anything save sufficient food to carry him to his next lodging. If he asks for money, he is a false prophet.*
>
> *It is by their conduct that the false prophet and the true prophet can be distinguished...Again, every prophet who*

teaches the truth but fails to practice what he preaches is a false prophet...If someone says in the Spirit, "Give me money, or something else," you must not heed him.

Everyone "who comes" to you "in the name of the Lord" must be welcomed. Afterward, when you have tested him, you will find out about him, for you have insight into right and wrong. --Early Christian Fathers, Vol. 1, Richardson, pg. 176-177.

Inside and Outside the Church

False ministries fall into two categories. The first category are false ministries from without or **from outside the church** (Acts 13:6; 20:29; Gal. 2:4).

Now when they had gone through the island to Paphos, they found a certain sorcerer, a false prophet, a Jew whose name was Bar-Jesus...

These ministries include representatives from false religions, fortune tellers, mediums, mystics and other such people (Lev. 19:31; 20:6, 27; Deut. 18:11-13). It is important to note that all those who are false prophets even from outside of the church claim to be functioning from the power of God. These ministries are not born again and their source is "the god of this world"—the devil. God warned His people about not participating with these falsities (Deut. 18:9-13). This is what He said as given to us in the Message Bible,

When you enter the land that GOD, your God, is giving you, don't take on the abominable ways of life of the nations there. Don't you dare sacrifice your son or daughter in the fire. Don't practice divination, sorcery, fortunetelling, witchery, casting spells, holding séances, or channeling with the dead. People who do these things are an abomination to GOD. It's because of just such abominable practices that GOD,

your God, is driving these nations out before you. Be completely loyal to GOD, your God.
Deuteronomy 18:9-13, Msg

To the mature believer these ministries are usually fairly easy to discern. Although often when they are accompanied by signs and wonders, even mature Christians can let their guard down (Acts 8:9-11). We have an example of this in the Book of Acts with a man called Simon Magnus who had been a sorcerer. Because he astonished the people with the miraculous, he was able to dupe them into believing that he was operating as God's agent.

But there was a certain man called Simon, who previously practiced sorcery in the city and astonished the people of Samaria, claiming that he was someone great, to whom they all gave heed, from the least to the greatest, saying, "This man is the great power of God." And they heeded him because he had astonished them with his sorceries for a long time.
Acts 8:9-11

The second category of false ministries are people who function from within or **from inside the church** (Mt. 7:15; Acts 20:30; 1 John 2:19). These come in sheep's clothing and are more difficult to spot. Both Jesus and Paul warned of these false ministries (Mt. 7:15; Acts 20:29-31).

Beware of false prophets, who come to you in sheep's clothing, but inwardly they are ravenous wolves.
Matthew 7:15

For I know this, that after my departure savage wolves will come in among you, not sparing the flock. ***Also from among yourselves men will rise up, speaking perverse things, to draw away the disciples after themselves.*** *Therefore watch, and remember that for three years I did not cease to warn everyone night and day with tears.* Acts 20:29-31

Evidently in Paul's experience, this issue of false ministry was so great that it was a rather constant part of his warning and admonition to the disciples in nearly all of his epistles.

Types of False Ministry

False ministries are of **various types** in the New Testament. The New Testament speaks of false apostles, false prophets, false shepherds or hirelings, false teachers, and false Christ's or anointed ones. Paul warns of **false apostles** in 2 Corinthians 11:13-15.

> *For such are **false apostles**, deceitful workers, transforming themselves into apostles of Christ. And no wonder! For Satan himself transforms himself into an angel of light. Therefore it is no great thing if his ministers also transform themselves into ministers of righteousness, whose end will be according to their works.* 2 Corinthians 11:13-15

A false apostle may claim to be a true apostle and may look to some degree like a true apostle, but in reality the false apostle is a person who is not as much interested in serving and laying down his or her life for others as a true apostle. A false apostle may have a completely different agenda.

Jesus commented the church at Ephesus because they were willing to test the apostles who made such claims to assay whether or not they were genuine (Rev. 2:2).

> *I know your works, your labor, your patience, and that you cannot bear those who are evil. And you have tested those who say they are apostles and are not, and have found them liars.* Revelation 2:2

False prophets are mentioned even more often than false apostles (Mt. 7:15; 24:11, 24; Mark 13:22; Acts 13:6; 2 Pet. 2: 1; 1 John 4:1). Just like the leaders at the church at Ephesus tested those who claimed to be apostles, John instructs us to test false prophets (1 John 4:1).

> *Beloved, do not believe every spirit, but test the spirits, whether they are of God; because many **false prophets** have gone out into the world.* 1 John 4:1

A false prophet may claim to be a true prophet and may look very much like a true prophet. The false prophet may even have prophecies that come to pass, but inwardly their heart is not right before the Lord. False prophets are inclined to tell you what you want to hear rather than what you need to hear so that they can be popular among the people (Jer. 5:31; 23:21; 29:8-9).

> *The prophets prophesy falsely, and the priests rule by their own power; and My people love to have it so. But what will you do in the end?* Jeremiah 5:31

> *The prophets prophesy lies, the priests rule by their own authority, and my people love it this way. But what will you do in the end?* –NIV

> *For thus says the LORD of hosts, the God of Israel: Do not let your prophets and your diviners who are in your midst deceive you, nor listen to your dreams which you cause to be dreamed. For they prophesy falsely to you in My name; I have not sent them, says the LORD.* Jeremiah 29:9

False shepherds or hirelings are referenced in both the Old and the New Testament (Jer. 23:1-5; Ezek. 34:1-10). Jesus contrasted His shepherding ministry with those that he labeled "hirelings" (John 10:11-13).

> *I am the good shepherd. The good shepherd gives His life for the sheep. But a hireling, he who is not the shepherd, one who does not own the sheep, sees the wolf coming and leaves the sheep and flees; and the wolf catches the sheep and scatters them. The hireling*

flees because he is a hireling and does not care about the sheep. John 10:11-13

A false shepherd may claim to be the man or woman of God, but in reality they care more about themselves and their own preservation or livelihood than they do about the flock of God. They function in the way that they do to gain something for themselves and when the fire gets hot, they do what is in their own best interest instead of what is best for the flock. Ezekiel records a stern warning from the Lord regarding false shepherds (I know it is long, but it is worth the read).

*Son of man, prophesy against the shepherds of Israel, prophesy and say to them, "thus says the Lord GOD to the shepherds: 'Woe to the shepherds of Israel **who feed themselves**! Should not the shepherds feed the flocks? 3 You eat the fat and clothe yourselves with the wool; you slaughter the fatlings, but you do not feed the flock. 4 The weak you have not strengthened, nor have you healed those who were sick, nor bound up the broken, nor brought back what was driven away, nor sought what was lost; but with force and cruelty you have ruled them. 5 So they were scattered because there was no shepherd; and they became food for all the beasts of the field when they were scattered. 6 My sheep wandered through all the mountains, and on every high hill; yes, My flock was scattered over the whole face of the earth, and no one was seeking or searching for them.' 7 Therefore, you shepherds, hear the word of the LORD: 8 'As I live,' says the Lord GOD, 'surely because My flock became a prey, and My flock became food for every beast of the field, because there was no shepherd, nor did My shepherds search for My flock, but the shepherds fed themselves and did not feed My flock'--9 therefore, O shepherds, hear the word of the LORD! 10 Thus says the Lord GOD: 'Behold, I am against the shepherds, and I will require My flock at their hand; I will cause them to cease feeding the sheep, and the shepherds shall feed themselves no more; for I will deliver My flock from* *their mouths, that they may no longer be food for them.'"* Ezekiel 34:1-10

False teachers were a big problem in the Early Church. Often these were itinerant preachers who went from place to place trying to peddle their unique take on things. This was common among Greek culture with would-be philosophers. These teachers were not really submitted to a particular local church but made their living by tickling the ears of those hungry for truth (1 Pet. 2:1; 1 Tim. 6:3-5).

*But there were also **false prophets** among the people, even as there will be **false teachers** among you, who will secretly bring in destructive heresies, even denying the Lord who bought them, and bring on themselves swift destruction.* 1 Peter 2:1

False teachers may look and sound very much like true teachers. The primary difference between them is the content of their teaching and the spirit with which they function. This doesn't mean that everything a false teacher teaches represents error. Quite the contrary, most of what a false teacher teaches is accurate. This is what can make it so difficult to discern.

Some false teachers may deny these things, but these are the sound, wholesome teachings of the Lord Jesus Christ, and they are the foundation for a godly life. Anyone who teaches anything different is both conceited and ignorant. Such a person has an unhealthy desire to quibble over the meaning of words. This stirs up arguments ending in jealousy, fighting, slander, and evil suspicions. These people always cause trouble. Their minds are corrupt, and they don't tell the truth. To them religion is just a way to get rich. 1 Timothy 6:3-5, NLT

Finally, Jesus spoke of **false christs** or "anointed ones" (Mt. 24:5, 24; Mark 13:22). You will notice that the word "christs" here is not capitalized. There is only one Christ who is worthy of capitalization and that is Jesus, the Christ of God. The word "Christ" is the Greek equivalent of the Hebrew word "Messiah." Both of these words literally mean "anointed one."

> *For false christs and false prophets will rise and show great signs and wonders to deceive, if possible, even the elect.* Matthew 24:24

One of the things that makes distinguishing between true and false ministries so difficult has to do with what is perceived to be their "anointing." Jesus indicated that there would be false "anointed ones" which suggests there is a false or counterfeit anointing.

This is why it is so important not to make a judgment about a ministry based on a feeling that you may have had in a meeting when they were speaking. God gives us other criteria for testing ministries which we will explore in later chapters.

Prevalent in the End Times

False ministries will be prevalent in the end times (Mt. 24:24-25; Mark 13:22; 1 Tim. 4:1; 2 Tim. 3:13). The word prevalent means "widespread, commonly occurring or practiced." False ministries will culminate in the manifestation of the "lawless one" and the false prophet who will have all power and manifest lying signs and wonders (2 Th. 2:1-12; 1 John 2:18; Rev. 13; 16:13-14; 19:20; 20:10).

While it is not our purpose in this book to discuss conflicting views of the end times, it is important to note that the Bible does speak of the antichrist and the false prophet coming forth to deceive. Whether these are actual people or spirits functioning through people is not our discussion. The point we are making here is that it is critical for us to realize that the closer we get to the return of the Lord the more important it is that we take these things seriously.

I close this chapter with a couple of key passages about the end times. I encourage you to prayerfully read through them. Following the verses you will find an appendix to this chapter that further describes the context in which the Church must shine in the end times.

2 Thessalonians 2:1-13, NLT

And now, brothers and sisters, let us tell you about the coming again of our Lord Jesus Christ and how we will be gathered together to meet him. 2 Please don't be so easily shaken and troubled by those who say that the day of the Lord has already begun. Even if they claim to have had a vision, a revelation, or a letter supposedly from us, don't believe them. 3 Don't be fooled by what they say. For that day will not come until there is a great rebellion against God and the man of lawlessness is revealed--the one who brings destruction. 4 He will exalt himself and defy every god there is and tear down every object of adoration and worship. He will position himself in the temple of God, claiming that he himself is God. 5 Don't you remember that I told you this when I was with you? 6 And you know what is holding him back, for he can be revealed only when his time comes. 7 For this lawlessness is already at work secretly, and it will remain secret until the one who is holding it back steps out of the way. 8 Then the man of lawlessness will be revealed, whom the Lord Jesus will consume with the breath of his mouth and destroy by the splendor of his coming. 9 This evil man will come to do the work of Satan with counterfeit power and signs and miracles. 10 He will use every kind of wicked deception to fool those who are on their way to destruction because they refuse to believe the truth that would save them. 11 So God will send great deception upon them, and they will believe all these lies. 12 Then they will be condemned for not believing the truth and for enjoying the evil they do. 13 As for us, we always thank God for you, dear brothers and sisters loved by the Lord. We are thankful that

God chose you to be among the first to experience salvation, a salvation that came through the Spirit who makes you holy and by your belief in the truth.

Revelation 13:11-14

Then I saw another beast coming up out of the earth, and he had two horns like a lamb and spoke like a dragon. And he exercises all the authority of the first beast in his presence and causes the earth and those who dwell in it to worship the first beast, whose deadly wound was healed. He performs great signs, so that he even makes fire come down from heaven on the earth in the sight of men. And he deceives those who dwell on the earth by those signs which he was granted to do in the sight of the beast, telling those who dwell on the earth to make an image to the beast who was wounded by the sword and lived.

Appendix 1, Lesson 2, The Context of the Last Days

We need to know our enemy. To be forewarned is to be forearmed. We are not to be those in darkness that the day should overtake up. The context in which the glorious church is to shine is described in **2 Timothy 3:1-5**.

Biblical Description	Synonyms	Antonyms
Lovers of Self	Fond of themselves, selfish, utterly self-centered	Selfless, considerate, others orientated
Covetous	Lovers of money, greedy, envious, motivated by money, grasping	Generous, liberal, self-sacrificing
Boasters	Full of big words, blow one's own horn, talk big, show off	Modest, accurate, grasping reality
Proud	Arrogant, conceited, insolent swagger, self-important, inflated, condescending, cocky, intolerant	Humble, lowly, submissive, unassuming, meek not weak
Blasphemers	Irreverent, profane, sacrilegious, cursing/swearing	Reverent, benevolent, pious
Disobedient to Parents	Rebellious to authority, disrespectful, obstinate, unmanageable, stubborn, defiant	Obedient, compliant, well behaved, manageable, submissive,
Unthankful	Thankless, inappreciative, critical	Appreciative, grateful, praising
Unholy	Worldly, wicked, corrupt, immoral, unsanctified, indecent, shameless	Spiritual, godly, moral, honest, virtuous, devout, righteous
Without Natural Affection	Unloving, hardhearted, callous, without familial love, insensitive	Caring, sympathetic, kind, warm-hearted
Trucebreakers	Irreconcilable, uncommitted, unforgiving	Conciliatory, loyal, committed, forgiving

False Accusers	Slanderers, malicious gossips, scandal-mongers, liars	Truthful, discreet, accurate, reliable, authentic, faithful
Incontinent	Lacking restraint or self-control, intemperate, given to excess, given to anger	Temperate, controlled, moderate, balanced, coolheaded, easygoing
Fierce	Savage, brutal, uncivilized, barbaric, cruel, sadistic, ruthless	Merciful, gentle, calm, peaceful, civilized, tender, compassionate
Despisers of the Good	Hateful, hostile to what is good, intolerant of those who practice good, enemies of decency	Promoters of good, lovers of good and those who practice that which is good.
Traitors	Betrayers, treacherous, faithless, devious, two-faced	Loyal, dependable, trustworthy, reliable, safe
Heady	Headstrong, reckless, defiant, adventurers, impulsive, rash, headlong with passion, hot-headed, bent on having one's own way, presumptuous	Manageable, cautious, cooperative, team player, principled, controlled
High-minded	Puffed up, lifted up in mind, swollen with self-importance	Humble, treating others with respect, valuing the contribution of others
Lovers of Pleasure	Feeling driven, love sensual and vain amusements, lives for the moment	Principle driven, driven by a passion to achieve destiny, able to see big picture
Having a form of godliness	Want to be perceived to be good, maintaining a religious facade, hypocritical, counterfeit, make-believe piety	True, proven, demonstrated, tested, tried, confirmed, real, substantial
Denying the Power of God	Stranger's to God's power, having no personal experience with God, resisting its influence in their lives	Their relationship to God is a living, vibrant part of all that they do. They live putting God in His rightful place.

Chapter 3
The Food and Fuel of False Ministries

To this point we have seen Jesus' warning about the potential for serious deception that will increase the closer we get to His Second Coming. We have seen that this deception will come through a variety of counterfeit ministries who can potentially come from both outside of the local church or inside of the local church. These ministries will include false apostles, false prophets, false pastors and false teachers. These ministries can carry a false anointing that makes it difficult to distinguish the true from the false.

One of the main reasons for writing this book is to make us aware of these ministries and to put tools in our hands to help us discern ministries and teachings that do not ring true when tested. In this chapter, I would like to talk about the food and the fuel of false ministry. When I say food or fuel, I am referring to what false ministries feed on or, should I say, who false ministries feed on or take advantage of.

The FOOD of False Ministries

We understand that for anyone to stay alive, they must eat. That means they have to be able to find food to sustain life. Food can be defined as "that which is eaten, diet or fodder." When we put this in the context of false ministries, the food of false ministries is sheep or God's people. Peter warned of such ministries in his second letter (See: 2 Pet. 2:2-3).

> *But there were also false prophets among the people, even as there will be false teachers among you, who will secretly bring in destructive heresies, even denying the Lord who bought them, and bring on themselves swift destruction. And many will follow their destructive ways, because of whom the way of truth will be blasphemed.* **By covetousness they will exploit you with deceptive words;** *for a long time their judgment has not been idle, and their destruction does not slumber.* 2 Peter 2:2-3

> *But there were also false prophets in Israel, just as there will be false teachers among you. They will cleverly teach their destructive heresies about God and even turn against their Master who bought them. Theirs will be a swift and terrible end. Many will follow their evil teaching and shameful immorality. And because of them, Christ and his true way will be slandered. In their greed they will make up clever lies to get hold of your money. But God condemned them long ago, and their destruction is on the way.* –NLT

False ministries prey on God's people and use them for their own self-seeking ends. However, it should be noted that they do not prey on just any sheep. Much like a wolf or other animals of prey they tend to go after the "easy pickings" or the "soft targets." One of our goals as believers is to take ourselves out of the "easy pickings" category.

The Bible speaks of five different categories of people that can become fodder for these ministries. *Firstly*, false ministries prey on the lambs or **new converts** (Amos 6:4; Eph. 4:14; 1 Tim. 3:6).

> *Then we will no longer be* **infants***, tossed back and forth by the waves, and blown here and there by every wind of teaching and by the cunning and craftiness of men in their deceitful scheming.* Ephesians 4:14, NIV

New converts are the immature in relationship to their faith and they know very little Scripture. In addition, they do not have a lot of experience with listening to the voice of God through an ongoing relationship with the Holy Spirit and the word of God. As a result, they do not yet know how to distinguish the voices of true and false shepherds. The more of a novice that someone is, the more susceptible they are to the pitfalls of the devil (1 Tim. 3:6).

Secondly, false ministries prey on the weak, immature and **ungrounded** (2 Pet. 2:14; 3:16). Peter speaks of these false teachers who bring in destructive heresies and who exploit people with deceptive words. In 2 Peter 2:13-15 he says,

*They are spots and blemishes, carousing in their own deceptions while they feast with you, 14 having eyes full of adultery and that cannot cease from sin, **enticing unstable souls**. They have a heart trained in covetous practices, and are accursed children. 15 They have forsaken the right way and gone astray, following the way of Balaam the son of Beor, who loved the wages of unrighteousness... 2 Peter 2:13b-15*

Verse 14 refers to the enticing, luring or seducing of "unstable souls." The word for "unstable" in the Greek means "unstable, vacillating or unfixed." These are people who are not fixed or established in their understanding or grounded enough in the word of God to be able to know the difference between truth and error.

*And so, dear friends, while you are waiting for these things to happen, make every effort to live a pure and blameless life. And be at peace with God. And remember, the Lord is waiting so that people have time to be saved. This is just as our beloved brother Paul wrote to you with the wisdom God gave him-- speaking of these things in all of his letters. Some of his comments are hard to understand, and those who are **ignorant and unstable** have twisted his letters around to mean something quite different from what*

> he meant, just as they do the other parts of Scripture-- **and the result is disaster for them.** 2 Peter 3:14-16, NLT

Thirdly, false ministries prey on the **gullible** and the needy or desperate (Rom. 16:18; 2 Tim. 3:6-7). Paul made reference to this in his letter to the Romans (16:18).

> *Now I urge you, brethren, note those who cause divisions and offenses, contrary to the doctrine which you learned, and avoid them. For those who are such do not serve our Lord Jesus Christ, but their own belly, and by smooth words and flattering speech they* ***deceive the hearts of the simple****.*
> Romans 16:17-18

> *I urge you, brothers and sisters, to watch out for those who cause divisions and put obstacles in your way that are contrary to the teaching you have learned. Keep away from them. For such people are not serving our Lord Christ, but their own appetites. By smooth talk and flattery* ***they deceive the minds of naive people****.*
> NIV

The word in this passage translated "simple" or "naïve" literally means those who are without guile, who are overly trusting with strangers and who never think ill of anyone. The New Living Translation refers to these people as "innocent."

> *Such people are not serving Christ our Lord; they are serving their own personal interests. By smooth talk and glowing words they deceive* ***innocent people****.*
> –NLT

Paul adds a bit more to this category in his second letter to Timothy.

> *For of this sort are those who creep into households and make captives of* ***gullible women*** *loaded down*

with sins, led away by various lusts, always learning and never able to come to the knowledge of the truth.
2 Timothy 3:6-7

Other translations translate this passage...

> *Weak-willed women...* --NIV
> *Vulnerable women...* --NLT

The Message Bible reads this way...

> *These are the kind of people who smooth-talk themselves into the homes of unstable and needy women and take advantage of them; women who, depressed by their sinfulness, take up with every new religious fad that calls itself "truth."*

It is important to understand that deception is not a women's or men's issue here. We are all vulnerable at times and, therefore, susceptible to deception. However, it must be said that women tend to have a more trusting nature that can often be exploited by those with impure motives in both the business and the church world. I know that this may seem a sexist thing to say, but just ask any auto mechanic.

Fourthly, false ministries prey on the **wounded and vulnerable** (Jer. 6:13-15). In the Old Testament Jeremiah identified such ministries.

> *"From the least to the greatest, they trick others to get what does not belong to them. Yes, even my prophets and priests are like that! They offer superficial treatments for my people's mortal wound. They give assurances of peace when all is war. Are they ashamed when they do these disgusting things? No, not at all--they don't even blush! Therefore, they will lie among the slaughtered. They will be humbled beneath my punishing anger," says the LORD.*
Jeremiah 6:13-15, NLT

The Message Bible says it this way,

"Everyone's after the dishonest dollar, little people and big people alike. Prophets and priests and everyone in between twist words and doctor truth. My people are broken--shattered! -- and they put on band-aids, Saying, 'It's not so bad. You'll be just fine.' But things are not 'just fine'! Do you suppose they are embarrassed over this outrage? No, they have no shame. They don't even know how to blush. There's no hope for them. They've hit bottom and there's no getting up. As far as I'm concerned, they're finished." GOD has spoken.

Finally, false ministries prey on **those who do not have a sincere love for the truth**. Paul wrote to the believers in Thessalonica regarding the coming of the lawless one (2 Th. 2:9-12).

The coming of the lawless one is according to the working of Satan, with all power, signs, and lying wonders, 10 and with all unrighteous deception among those who perish, because **they did not receive the love of the truth***, that they might be saved. 11 And for this reason God will send them strong delusion, that they should believe the lie, 12 that they all may be condemned who did not believe the truth but had pleasure in unrighteousness.*
2 Thessalonians 2:9-12

Other translations say...

...but they will refuse to love the truth and accept it.
– CEV

...they refused to love the truth. – NIV

...they did not welcome into their hearts the love of the truth. – Wuest

There are many people who do not want to hear the truth. This is true in the natural world, but it can also be true in the church. Rather than the truth, they want to hear words that will make them feel good about themselves. And there are plenty of so-called ministries that will give them what they want.

Jeremiah had a word from the Lord that involved returning to the Lord with repentance. Other prophets were leading people to believe that everything was fine. But the truth is that Jeremiah had the actual word of the Lord while the other prophets were leading the people astray. It is through speaking the truth in love that we grow up to be mature believers (Eph. 4:15).

Sheep are Vulnerable

When God speaks of His people, he puts them into the context of sheep needing shepherds. God could have chosen any animal to serve as an illustration of His people but He chose sheep (See: Num. 27:17; 1 Kgs. 22:17; 2 Chr. 18:16; Zech. 10:2; Mt. 9:36; John 10:14, 27). I believe that He created sheep with these qualities specifically to tell us something about ourselves. This is, on the one hand, very unflattering and, one the other hand, quite flattering. This imagery has two aspects to it—one negative and one positive.

On the negative side, sheep are very needy. Sheep are especially needy for three reasons. Firstly sheep do not have an ability to find food on their own (Num. 27:16-17). Sheep are not like other foraging animals that will send out scouts and lead the herd to food. It is said that sheep will die in a pasture that has been grazed out with fresh pasture right over the next hill. Sheep must be led to their food.

Secondly, sheep do not seem to have an instinct to return home. Their tendency is to go astray (Ezek. 34:6-8). Sheep have never been known to be able to find their way home if they are lost. Dogs and other animals can often do this. However, the nature of sheep is to make all of the wrong choices when it comes to guidance, so they will need someone to lead them back to the safety of the fold.

The third negative about sheep it that they have no real natural defense system. Domestic sheep have no claws, sharp teeth, powerful jaws, or incredible speed and are not known for their great strength. These are some of nature's means of defense for many animals. Their only real defense is their ability to flock. As they stick together under the leadership of the shepherd they are less vulnerable to an attack from a wild animal. I have been told that if sheep are not sheared regularly, they can actually become wool-bound and can potentially die when they fall over, being too heavy to get back up.

This is the picture that God paints of His people. One naturally has to ask the question, "Are they worth it?" God's answer is, "YES!" On the positive side, sheep were always considered very valuable. They were valuable to the shepherd because they could provide most of man's needs including food (meat, cheese), drink (milk) and clothing (wool).

False ministries exploit the nature and the defenselessness of sheep. Paul noted this in his letter to the Galatians (Gal. 1:6-7).

> *I am shocked that you are turning away so soon from God, who in his love and mercy called you to share the eternal life he gives through Christ. You are already following a different way that pretends to be the Good News but is not the Good News at all. You are being fooled by those who twist and change the truth concerning Christ.* Galatians 1:6-7, NLT

The Appetite of Sheep (Believers)

When it comes to a change of direction from the right way to the wrong way sheep can stray very quickly. Paul speaks of these believers being "rapidly, quickly or speedily" drawn away from the truth. We have already seen how sheep are prone to wander (Is 53:6a). But there are other characteristics of believers as God's sheep that can set them up or tee them up for false ministries to exploit. The New Testament identifies four such characteristics that deal with our appetites as believers.

The first characteristic of God's people as sheep is that they have **an appetite for the sensational**. Earlier we discussed how the people of Samaria were under the spell of Simon Magnus because of all the miraculous things that he did. When they saw these things they fully believed that he was God's messenger (Acts 8:18-10).

Paul and Barnabas had a similar experience when they went to Lystra (Acts 14:8-20). When they came into the city and healed a lame man, the people saw what they did and immediately assumed they were gods who had come down from heaven. Here is their story...

And in Lystra a certain man without strength in his feet was sitting, a cripple from his mother's womb, who had never walked. 9 This man heard Paul speaking. Paul, observing him intently and seeing that he had faith to be healed, 10 said with a loud voice, "Stand up straight on your feet!" And he leaped and walked. 11 Now when the people saw what Paul had done, they raised their voices, saying in the Lycaonian language, "The gods have come down to us in the likeness of men!"12 And Barnabas they called Zeus, and Paul, Hermes, because he was the chief speaker.13 Then the priest of Zeus, whose temple was in front of their city, brought oxen and garlands to the gates, intending to sacrifice with the multitudes.14 But when the apostles Barnabas and Paul heard this, they tore their clothes and ran in among the multitude, crying out 15 and saying, "Men, why are you doing these things? We also are men with the same nature as you and preach to you that you should turn from these useless things to the living God, who made the heaven, the earth, the sea, and all things that are in them,16 who in bygone generations allowed all nations to walk in their own ways. 17 Nevertheless He did not leave Himself without witness, in that He did good, gave us rain from heaven and fruitful seasons, filling our hearts with food and gladness."18 And with these sayings they could scarcely restrain the multitudes from sacrificing to them. Acts 14:8-1

Because these men performed a miracle the crowds were ready to proclaim them as gods. Only a few verses later they were persuaded by others to stone these messengers. Does the phrase "fickle followers" come to mind?

Then Jews from Antioch and Iconium came there; and having persuaded the multitudes, they stoned Paul and dragged him out of the city, supposing him to be dead. However, when the disciples gathered around him, he rose up and went into the city. And the next day he departed with Barnabas to Derbe. Acts 14:19-20

If people are drawn by the sensational, they will always want the more and the more sensational if they are to remain loyal.

The second characteristic of God's people as sheep is that they have a thirst or an **appetite for that which is new** or novel. Paul makes reference to this in his second letter to his spiritual son, Timothy (2 Tim. 4:3-4).

For the time will come when they will not endure sound doctrine, but according to their own desires, because they have itching ears, they will heap up for themselves teachers; and they will turn their ears away from the truth, and be turned aside to fables.
2 Timothy 4:3-4

Somehow in the culture of our times, we have this idea that "new" is the same thing as "better." I have seen people who were willing to get any new car rather than getting an older, but more reliable car.

People get bored with the old. And yet when it comes to doctrine, it is dangerous to always be looking for a new doctrine or a new revelation. Sometimes the "new" things are the equivalent of "fables." Fables are fictional inventions of people. The word of God has power because it is God's word and has not been invented for the purpose of gaining a following.

Contrast the Berean believers in Acts 17:11 and the Athenians in Acts 17:21. The Bereans listened with an open skepticism that was willing to search out what was being taught to ensure that it was indeed scriptural. The Athenians treated the exposition of doctrine like a sport and were only looking for something new or novel that they could enjoy.

> *Then the brethren immediately sent Paul and Silas away by night to Berea. When they arrived, they went into the synagogue of the Jews. These were more fair-minded than those in Thessalonica, in that they received the word with all readiness, and searched the Scriptures daily to find out whether these things were so. Therefore many of them believed, and also not a few of the Greeks, prominent women as well as men.*
> Acts 17:10-12

> *And they took him and brought him to the Areopagus, saying, "May we know what this new doctrine is of which you speak? For you are bringing some strange things to our ears. Therefore we want to know what these things mean." For all the Athenians and the foreigners who were there spent their time in nothing else but either to tell them or to hear some new thing.*
> Acts 17:19-21

The third characteristic of God's people as sheep is that **they love private, mysterious or secret interpretation**, revelation or experience (Mt. 24:26-27; 2 Pet.1:20; 2:1).

> *Then if anyone says to you, "Look, here is the Christ!" or "There!" do not believe it. 24 For false christs and*

> *false prophets will rise and show great signs and wonders to deceive, if possible, even the elect. 25 See, I have told you beforehand. 26 Therefore if they say to you, "Look, He is in the desert!" do not go out; or "Look, He is in the inner rooms!" do not believe it.*
> Matthew 24:23-26

It is interesting that Jesus uses the term "inner rooms" here. So often those who seek to infiltrate the church with their questionable teachings call people to some "secret place." False ministries love to operate in secret to avoid detection by the true leaders of the flock. They use secret meetings with special invitations often assembled under false pretenses without the knowledge or approval of local church leadership.

> *But there were also false prophets among the people, even as there will be false teachers among you, who will secretly bring in destructive heresies, even denying the Lord who bought them, and bring on themselves swift destruction.* 2 Peter 2:1

The fourth characteristic of God's people as sheep is that **they love to hear what they want to hear** (Jer. 5:31). They are not as concerned about what they need to hear as they are what they want to hear. They are wanting a word that is non-confrontational, does not require any change on their part, makes them feel good about themselves and, as a bonus, is entertaining.

> *The prophets prophesy falsely, and the priests rule by their own power; and My people love to have it so. But what will you do in the end?*

Albert Barnes suggests that this could be read, "the priests govern according to their false prophecies, guidance, and directions." And the people love it because their words do not really challenge them to change. Barnes adds, "False teaching lightens the yoke of God's Law, and removes His fear from the conscience: and with this, man is ready to be content."

Paul eventually said to some of his followers in essence, "If I tell you the truth will you hate me?" What he literally said was, *"Have I therefore become your enemy because I tell you the truth?* (Gal. 4:16).

The people wanted to kill Jesus because He spoke a truth that they did not want to hear (John 8:40).

But now you seek to kill Me, a Man who has told you the truth which I heard from God. Abraham did not do this. John 8:40

Paul indicated that the time would come when people would not endure sound doctrine (2 Tim. 4:3a). It will not be enough for them, they will want new, spectacular, private and pleasant to the taste.

For the time will come when they will not endure sound doctrine... 2 Timothy 4:3

This word for "sound" literally means "that which is healthy or that which is good for you." Too many people are like children who want to eat things that are bad for them and things that will lead them into a state of sickness.

It is interesting in the natural that many of the exotic foods that people crave are not really that good for you. Some of them if prepared improperly can actually kill you. God has some basic food for us which will cause us to prosper and be in health spiritually. We must be careful that we never lose our appetite for the basics or that which gives and sustains life.

The FUEL of false ministries

The food and the fuel of false ministries are similar concepts using different analogies. When we talk about fuel, we are talking about things that fuel the fire. Fuel is defined as whatever feeds or sustains any expenditure, outlay, passion or excitement. False ministries are fueled by dry tinder. This includes people who are:

1. Discontent
2. Downcast
3. Discouraged
4. Desperate

False ministries actually look for such people that they can reach out to with compassion and understanding. They often pit themselves against local church leaders who do not or cannot care for them or help them like they can. There are always plenty of people like this in most churches. It is rarely because of there is non-caring leadership in the local assembly, it is more often that they are not willing or able to tap into what is available to them.

False ministries are fueled by **wrong inner desires and motivation**. Many of these false ministries care about themselves more than they do the sheep (Rom. 16:18; John 10:13; Phil. 3:19; Ezek. 34:2-3, 8).

Brethren, join in following my example, and note those who so walk, as you have us for a pattern. For many walk, of whom I have told you often, and now tell you even weeping, that they are the enemies of the cross of Christ: whose end is destruction, whose god is their belly, and whose glory is in their shame--who set their mind on earthly things. Philippians 3:17-19

In the above passage, when Paul speaks of those whose "god is their belly," he means that there are those who serve their own appetites and preach doctrines which cater to the fulfillment of their own natural passions. These are those who are in the ministry for the purpose of attaining earthly things.

False ministries can be further fueled by **selfish ambition** (Phil. 1:16). They have a desire for acclaim, position, power or control.

Some indeed preach Christ even from envy and strife, and some also from goodwill: The former preach Christ from selfish ambition, not sincerely, supposing to add affliction to my chains... Philippians 1:15-16

False ministries can also be fueled by a **spirit of covetousness** (1 Tim. 6:5-10; Tit. 1:11; 2 Peter 2:3). In other words...they want your money and your possessions. They use their gifts to manipulate people into giving money directly to them.

Anyone who teaches anything different is both conceited and ignorant. Such a person has an unhealthy desire to quibble over the meaning of words. This stirs up arguments ending in jealousy, fighting, slander, and evil suspicions. 5 These people always cause trouble. Their minds are corrupt, and they don't tell the truth. To them religion is just a way to get rich. 6 Yet true religion with contentment is great wealth. 7 After all, we didn't bring anything with us when we came into the world, and we certainly cannot carry anything with us when we die. 8 So if we have enough food and clothing, let us be content. 9 But people who long to be rich fall into temptation and are trapped by many foolish and harmful desires that plunge them into ruin and destruction. 10 For the love of money is at the root of all kinds of evil. And some people, craving money, have wandered from the faith and pierced themselves with many sorrows. 1 Timothy 6:4-10, NLT

Many will follow their evil teaching and shameful immorality. And because of them, Christ and his true way will be slandered. In their greed they will make up clever lies to get hold of your money. But God condemned them long ago, and their destruction is on the way. 2 Peter 2:2-3, NLT

Finally, false ministries can be fueled by **a desire for a following** (Acts 20:29-30).

For I know this, that after my departure savage wolves will come in among you, not sparing the flock. Also from among yourselves men will rise up, speaking perverse things, to draw away the disciples after themselves. Acts 20:29-31

The New Living Translation says, "*Even some of you will distort the truth in order to draw a following.*"

There are some people who are not motivated by money, fame or worldly pleasures but who are extremely motivated with the potential to have a following, even if only a very few people follow them. Often they create a unique and very, disciplined message to create a band of radical disciples who will follow them anywhere...even to death.

Summary

It should be quite apparent that the issue of false ministry was taken very seriously by the New Testament writers. Not all such ministry is easy to identify and many such ministries may not even realize that they fall into this category. We now know that we are all vulnerable both as victims and perpetrators of false ministry.

God is very jealous over His people. He loves the sheep of His pasture and He is very troubled when He sees them taken advantage of. He is particularly troubled when He sees the newborn babes, the weak in the faith, the wounded and other hurting sheep abused.

In the next chapter we will be looking at the face of false ministry. False ministry does not present itself as false ministry.

Chapter 4
The Face, Fruit and Fate of False Ministries

In this book we are addressing the issue of discernment. We are addressing the issue of the need for such discernment, especially as we get closer to the return of the Lord when Jesus tells us that we will see a rise of false ministries who have the potential of leading us astray. Why do we need such discernment? We need it because false ministries do not present themselves as such. They look very much like the real and can have a false anointing that can resemble the true anointing. How do false ministries present themselves? What is the face of false ministry?

The FACE of False Ministries

The word "face" refers to the surface of anything. It refers to the front. It refers to the side or edge that is presented to view. When we apply this to false ministry, we are referring to how they present themselves or how they are viewed by all outward appearances.

On the outside (the face), false ministries seem to have a positive appeal. Paul indicates that they often speak smooth, persuasive and flattering words or blessings (Rom. 16:18; Col. 2 4).

...smooth words and flattering speech... Rom. 16:18b

...smooth talk and glowing words... --NLT

Barnes says that these people make "mild, fair, plausible speeches; with an appearance of great sincerity, and regard for the truth." In addition they use flattery to entice people.

Now this I say lest anyone should deceive you with persuasive words. Colossians 2:4

I tell you this so that no one may deceive you by fine-sounding arguments.

The word used for "deceive" in this Colossian passage is a word that means to mislead by false reasoning or argument. False ministries depend on average Christians not knowing their Bibles well and not being grounded in theology. This is a perfect set up so that they can mislead them.

Just like the devil, false ministries present themselves as angels of light and ministers of righteousness (2 Cor. 11:13-15).

For such are false apostles, deceitful workers, transforming themselves into apostles of Christ. And no wonder! For Satan himself **transforms himself into an angel of light.** *Therefore it is no great thing if his ministers also transform themselves into ministers of righteousness, whose end will be according to their works.* 2 Corinthians 11:13-15

In the above passage, Paul refers to false apostles who have transformed themselves into apostles of Christ. Often people like this push the idea of their apostleship and expect others to acknowledge it as well. Often they do not answer to anyone. It is as if they have laid hands on their own heads and have ordained themselves?

False ministries often claim to be somebody (Mt. 24:5; John 5:43). They can make all kinds of claims for themselves which cannot always be substantiated by reality or their ministry fruit. Jesus said many will come in His name claiming, "*I am the Christ,*" and many will be deceived by their claims (Mt. 24:5). They are not claiming to be "The Christ," but they are claiming to be anointed like Christ.

You might ask, "What kind of claims might they make?" Here are a few things that they may claim.

- They may claim to have answers that your elders do not have.
- They may claim to hear directly from God.
- They may claim that God has given them a key that only the very spiritual can understand.

In addition, false ministries can superficially heal people with a message of peace (Jer. 6:13-15). False ministries speak of peace and safety (Ezek. 13:10, 16). God warns false ministries through the mouth of Ezekiel.

> *I will raise My fist against all the prophets who see **false visions** and make **lying predictions**, and they will be banished from the community of Israel. I will blot their names from Israel's record books, and they will never again set foot in their own land. Then you will know that I am the Sovereign LORD. This will happen because these evil prophets deceive My people by saying, 'All is peaceful' when there is no peace at all!* Ezekiel 13:9-10a, New Living Translation

They speak peace and safety because to speak what people really need to heal them to the core would not always be popular and would not always return to them tangibly (Jer. 8:10-12).

> "From the least to the greatest, they trick others to get what does not belong to them. Yes, even my prophets and priests are like that! They offer superficial treatments for my people's mortal wound. They give assurances of peace when all is war. Are they ashamed when they do these disgusting things? No, not at all--they don't even blush! Therefore, they will lie among the slaughtered. They will be humbled beneath my punishing anger," says the LORD.
>
> Jeremiah 8:10b-12, NLT

Characteristics of False Ministry

False ministries may present themselves as true anointed ones, they may even believe their own advertising, but on the inside or in the background things are not so appealing. The New Testament mentions nine different characteristics of false ministry. While no one ministry is likely to have all nine, it is good to be cautioned by them.

1. False ministries draw disciples to themselves rather than leading them to local church leadership (Acts 20:30). They lead people away from God-ordained committed relationships.

   > *I know that after I leave, that savage wolves will come in among you and will not spare the flock. Even from your own number men will arise and distort the truth **in order to draw away disciples** after them.*
   >
   > Acts 20:29-39, NIV

2. False ministries speak misleading things and distortions of the Gospel (Gal 1:7; Acts 20:30).

   > *I marvel that you are turning away so soon from Him who called you in the grace of Christ, to a different gospel, 7 which is not another; but there are some who trouble you and want to pervert the gospel of Christ. 8 But even if we, or an angel from heaven, preach any other gospel to you than what we have preached to*

you, let him be accursed. 9 As we have said before, so now I say again, if anyone preaches any other gospel to you than what you have received, let him be accursed. 10 For do I now persuade men, or God? Or do I seek to please men? For if I still pleased men, I would not be a bondservant of Christ. Galatians 1:6-10

*I am astonished that you are so quickly deserting the one who called you by the grace of Christ and are turning to a different gospel--which is really no gospel at all. Evidently some people are throwing you into confusion and are trying to **pervert the gospel** of Christ.* Galatians 1:6-7, NIV

This passage speaks of those who "pervert" the Gospel. To pervert is to twist, turn around and change the meaning.

3. False ministries practice deceit by teaching fabricated or forged words (not being totally honest with themselves or others) (2 Pet. 2:3a).

   *By **covetousness** they will **exploit** you with **deceptive** words...* 2 Pet. 2:3a

   There are three words used by Peter in the above passage that fill out the meaning for us. The three words are "covetousness, exploit and deceptive." The word *covetousness* is a word that means a greedy desire to get more. The word *exploit* is a word that means to use a person or thing for gain. The word *deceptive* is a word that is used only here in the Bible and literally means molded out of wax or clay.

   This word for deceptive can refer to carefully molded and crafted words used to manipulate people to attain their covetous desires. These are words that are constructed on the spot for this occasion and for a specific purpose. But like wax they will not endure the heat.

4. False ministries have spiritual pride, believing and leading people to believe that they have secret revelation that only comes through them (1 Tim. 6:3-5).

If anyone teaches otherwise and does not consent to wholesome words, even the words of our Lord Jesus Christ, and to the doctrine which accords with godliness, he is proud, knowing nothing, but is obsessed with disputes and arguments over words, from which come envy, strife, reviling, evil suspicions, useless wranglings of men of corrupt minds and destitute of the truth, who suppose that godliness is a means of gain. From such withdraw yourself.
1 Timothy 6:3-5

5. False ministries speak evil of things that they do not fully understand (1 Tim. 6:3-5; 2 Pet. 2:12, 17; Jude 10).

Peter says that these false ministries are like "wells without water" (2 Pet. 2:17). False ministries like to give you the perception that they are deep, but when you get to the bottom there is "no water."

6. False ministries are obsessed with disputes and arguments over words (1 Tim. 6:4).

7. False ministries see godliness as a means of gain (1 Tim. 6:5).

8. False ministries will preach a message of peace with no mention of repentance (Jer. 6:13-15).

9. False ministries teach that their message brings liberty while they themselves are slaves of corruption (2 Pet. 2:18-19).

For when they speak great swelling words of emptiness, they allure through the lusts of the flesh, through lewdness, the ones who have actually escaped from those who live in error. While they promise them liberty, they themselves are slaves of corruption; for by whom a person is overcome, by him also he is brought into bondage. 2 Peter 2:18-19

The FRUIT of False Ministries

The word "fruit" speaks of the consequence or result of any action. It refers to any outcome, effect, result; aftermath, the product or production of something. What kind of fruit do these false ministries produce? What is the result of their ministry? What remains when they are done? What do they leave in their wake? Jesus warned us in Matthew that good trees bear good fruit, but bad trees cannot produce good, long-lasting fruit.

Beware of false prophets, who come to you in sheep's clothing, but inwardly they are ravenous wolves. 16 You will know them by their fruits. Do men gather grapes from thornbushes or figs from thistles? 17 Even so, every good tree bears good fruit, but a bad tree bears bad fruit. 18 A good tree cannot bear bad fruit, nor can a bad tree bear good fruit. 19 Every tree that does not bear good fruit is cut down and thrown into the fire. 20 Therefore by their fruits you will know them. Matthew 7:15-20

The Bible speaks to the subject of fruit when it comes to false ministries. I have identified some of the things that could fall into this category. The first negative fruit of false ministry is that they do not lead people to true repentance. God addressed this through His prophet Jeremiah. He spoke of the ministries as living in compromise themselves and never really challenging their listeners to change their lives and repent (Jer. 23:14, 21-22).

I did not send these prophets, yet they have run with their message; I did not speak to them, yet they have prophesied. But if they had stood in my council, they would have proclaimed my words to my people and would have turned them from their evil ways and from their evil deeds. Jeremiah 23:21-22

The second negative aspect of the fruit of false ministries is that, since they do not challenge people's lifestyle and live a compromised lifestyle themselves, it actually strengthens the hands of evil doers. It becomes easy for people to say that if these ministries can live this way, then it must be alright for me to do so as well (Jer. 23:14).

And among the prophets of Jerusalem I have seen something horrible: They commit adultery and live a lie. They strengthen the hands of evildoers, so that no one turns from his wickedness. They are all like Sodom to me; the people of Jerusalem are like Gomorrah. Jeremiah 23:14, NIV

The third negative fruit of false ministries is that they cause people to stray and they lead them into err (Jer. 23:13, 32; Mic. 3:5).

"Behold, I am against those who prophesy false dreams," says the LORD, "and tell them, and cause My people to err by their lies and by their recklessness. Yet I did not send them or command them; therefore they shall not profit this people at all," says the LORD. Jeremiah 23:32

This is what the LORD says to you false prophets: "You are leading my people astray! You promise peace for those who give you food, but you declare war on anyone who refuses to pay you." Micah 3:5

The fourth negative fruit of false ministries is that they make people worthless (Jer. 23:16-17).

Thus says the LORD of hosts: "Do not listen to the words of the prophets who prophesy to you. They make you worthless; they speak a vision of their own heart, not from the mouth of the LORD. They continually say to

those who despise Me, 'The LORD has said, "You shall have peace"; and to everyone who walks according to the dictates of his own heart, they say, 'No evil shall come upon you.'"

The word for "worthless" here can mean that they "fill you with vain hopes." Gill says, "They filled their heads with vain and empty things, and their hearts with vain hopes, which deceived them." Because they have their heads "in the clouds," it is difficult for them to deal with reality and truly see themselves as God sees them and truly embrace whom God has made them to be.

The fifth negative fruit of false ministries is that they cause people to neglect God and His word (Jer. 23:22, 27).

"I have heard these prophets say, 'Listen to the dream I had from God last night.' And then they proceed to tell lies in my name. 26 How long will this go on? If they are prophets, they are prophets of deceit, inventing everything they say. 27 By telling these false dreams, they are trying to get my people to forget me, just as their ancestors did by worshiping the idols of Baal. 28 Let these false prophets tell their dreams, but let my true messengers faithfully proclaim my every word. There is a difference between chaff and wheat! 29 Does not my word burn like fire?" asks the LORD. "Is it not like a mighty hammer that smashes rock to pieces?" 30 "Therefore," says the LORD, "I stand against these prophets who get their messages from each other--31 these smooth-tongued prophets who say, 'This prophecy is from the LORD!' 32 Their imaginary dreams are flagrant lies that lead my people into sin. I did not send or appoint them, and they have no message at all for my people," says the LORD.   Jeremiah 23:25-32, NLT

False ministries want people to be dependent on them rather than teaching them to receive directly from God through a personal relationship with Him. They spend all of their time preaching from their latest dream or angelic visitation rather than the Word of God.

Bad Fruit in the Local Church

In addition to the negative fruit in the lives of vulnerable people, the fruit of false ministries as it relates to the local church is also bad. As a rule they are more interested in building their ministry and a personal following than they are in building the local church. They are more interested in garnering support for themselves and often do so by undermining local leadership and forcing people to choose where their loyalties lie.

There are some common attributes of these ministries as it relate to local church where they may attend (for a season).

1. False ministries often **cause division and strife** (Rom. 16:17).

   Now I urge you, brethren, note those who cause divisions and offenses, contrary to the doctrine which you learned, and avoid them.

   They do this by sowing discord among the saint by offering then a different "take" on the things that church leaders have been teaching. Notice that the divisions and offenses referred to in the above passage have to do with the doctrine or teachings of the local church.

   And now I make one more appeal, my dear brothers and sisters. Watch out for people who cause divisions and upset people's faith by teaching things that are contrary to what you have been taught. Stay away from them. –NLT

2. False ministries are **a source of constant friction** (I Tim. 6:3-5, NIV).

> *If anyone teaches false doctrines and does not agree to the sound instruction of our Lord Jesus Christ and to godly teaching, he is conceited and understands nothing. He has an unhealthy interest in controversies and quarrels about words that result in envy, strife, malicious talk, evil suspicions and constant friction between men of corrupt mind, who have been robbed of the truth and who think that godliness is a means to financial gain.*

Notice the negative fruit referred to in this passage includes...

- Controversies
- Quarrels (about meaningless things)
- Envy
- Strife
- Malicious Talk
- Evil Suspicions
- Constant Friction

3. False ministries **unsettle souls** (Acts 15:24).

> *Since we have heard that some who went out from us have troubled you with words, unsettling your souls, saying, "You must be circumcised and keep the law" --to whom we gave no such commandment...*

There are two words in this passage that describe the fruit of false ministries in the local church. First of all, false ministries "trouble" the souls of people. The word "trouble" in this passage means to cause inner commotion, to take away peace of mind and to make restless through anxiety or fear. I suppose telling a whole room full of Gentiles that they needed to be circumcised to be saved would cause a little restlessness.

The second word in the above passage that describes the fruit of false ministries in the local church is that they "unsettle" people. The word "unsettle" in this passage means to subvert, undermine and to dismantle. False teachers unsettle people by undermining the leadership of the local church and calling into question many of the solid foundations of Christian doctrine so that people are no longer sure of what they believe. True ministries are builders not dismantlers.

4. False ministries **do not profit** the people of God (Jer. 23:32, NIV).

> *"Indeed, I am against those who prophesy false dreams," declares the LORD. "They tell them and lead my people astray with their reckless lies, yet I did not send or appoint them. They do not benefit these people in the least," declares the LORD.*

The FATE of False Ministries

We do not use the word "fate" very often, but the word "fate" essentially means destiny. It is their lot or their predetermined outcome. God is a very jealous God and He is particularly jealous when it comes to His children. Jesus is particularly jealous when it comes to His Bride—the Church.

As a result, God has a very negative view of false ministry. When you mess with a man's children or his wife you incur his wrath. When you mess with the Church you are messing with the wife of Jesus. You better watch out!

God makes it clear that He sees false ministers as abominable (Jer. 5:30-31; 23:14).

> *An astonishing and horrible thing has been committed in the land: The prophets prophesy falsely, and the priests rule by their own power; and My people love to have it so.* Jeremiah 5:30-31

An appalling and horrible thing... --Amp
A horrible and shocking thing... --NLT

He sees false ministers as spots and blemishes (2 Pet. 2:13b-14; Jude 12-13).

They are spots and blemishes, carousing in their own deceptions while they feast with you, having eyes full of adultery and that cannot cease from sin, enticing unstable souls. They have a heart trained in covetous practices, and are accursed children.
2 Peter 2:13b-14

The word that is used for "blemish" here can also be translated "disgrace." These false ministers are a disgrace to the Gospel.

When these people join you in fellowship meals celebrating the love of the Lord, they are like dangerous reefs that can shipwreck you. They are shameless in the way they care only about themselves. They are like clouds blowing over dry land without giving rain, promising much but producing nothing. They are like trees without fruit at harvesttime. They are not only dead but doubly dead, for they have been pulled out by the roots. They are like wild waves of the sea, churning up the dirty foam of their shameful deeds. They are wandering stars, heading for everlasting gloom and darkness.
Jude 12-13

In the above passage, Jude refers to these false ministries as...

- Dangerous reefs that can cause shipwreck
- Shameless
- Clouds without rain (there is the expectation of refreshment but only disappointment)

- Trees without fruit at harvest time (there is expectation of fruit but none to be found)
- Dead and doubly dead
- Wild waves churning up dirty foam
- Wandering stars headed for destruction

Because of this, God will ultimately judge false ministries (Jer. 14:14-15; 23:15; 2 Cor. 11:15; 2 Pet. 2:17). The Message Bible renders 2 Corinthians 11:15 this way,

So it shouldn't surprise us when his servants masquerade as servants of God. But they're not getting by with anything. They'll pay for it in the end.

And, just how does God say that He will bring judgment upon them. Here are five things that God says that He will do in relation to false ministries.

1. He will take His people out of their hands (Ezek. 34:10).

This is what the Sovereign LORD says: I now consider these shepherds my enemies, and I will hold them responsible for what has happened to my flock. I will take away their right to feed the flock, along with their right to feed themselves. I will rescue my flock from their mouths; the sheep will no longer be their prey. –NLT

2. He will remove their prophetic revelation (Mic. 3:5-7).

This is what the LORD says to you false prophets: "You are leading my people astray! You promise peace for those who give you food, but you declare war on anyone who refuses to pay you. 6 Now the night will close around you, cutting off all your visions. Darkness will cover you, making it impossible for you to predict the future. The sun will set for you prophets, and your day will come to an end. 7 Then you seers will cover your faces in shame, and you diviners will be disgraced. And you will admit that your messages were not from God."

3. He will no longer respond to their cry (Mic. 3:7, NIV).

   The seers will be ashamed and the diviners disgraced. They will all cover their faces because there is no answer from God.

4. He will bring swift destruction upon them (2 Pet. 2:1, 3).

   But there were also false prophets among the people, just as there will be false teachers among you. They will secretly introduce destructive heresies, even denying the sovereign Lord who bought them-- bringing swift destruction on themselves.   1 Peter 2:1

Chapter 5
Keeping Ourselves Pure

After doing the last four chapters on the challenges of identifying false ministries, it is important that we not assume for a minute that we could not enter into deception ourselves and become one of those ministries. People who function as false ministries rarely know that they are actually false. Most people who function as false ministries are self-deceived and believe in themselves and what they are doing. That is why they can be so convincing.

So how does one ensure that he or she stays true to God, to His word and to the call that God has on his or her life? How can I keep myself from deception in days of "strong delusion"?

Examining My Heart

Jesus challenged people, who were in a position to speak into the lives of others concerning what they perceived to be their faults, to check themselves out first (Mt. 7:3-5). Paul encouraged the elders at Ephesus to examine or "take heed" to themselves as their first responsibility in leading others. People who purport to be leaders need to start with a little self-examination (Acts 20:28).

Leaders must be willing to start by examining their own hearts. King David understood this as he prayed to God to help him in this endeavor (Ps. 139:23-24).

> *Search me, O God, and know my heart; test me and know my thoughts. Point out anything in me that offends you, and lead me along the path of everlasting life.* Psalm 139:23-24, NLT

Jesus was able to say in John 14:30:

> *I will no longer talk much with you, for the ruler of this world is coming, and he has nothing in Me.*

Other translations render Jesus' statement as follows:

> *...he has no hold on Me.* –NIV
>
> *...he has nothing in common with Me.* –TCNT
>
> *...he has no claim on Me.* –Beck
>
> *...there is nothing in Me that belongs to him.* –Amp
>
> *...there is nothing in Me that responds to him.* –Ukn
>
> *But don't worry—he has nothing on me, no claim on me.* –Msg

Leaders must know their own hearts. They must be willing to be honest with themselves and be willing to analyze the reasons why they are in the ministry. They must be willing to be honest about the things that truly motivate them.

Some questions leaders can ask themselves to assist in this self-examination process include the following:

1. What are my heart attitudes?

2. What are my motivations?

3. Is there anything in me that Satan can use for his ends?

4. Why am I in the ministry?

   Am I in leadership ministry...

- To make a name for myself?
- To be great in man's eyes?
- To have a following?
- To please or impress men?
- To be in the limelight?
- To have position and power over the lives of people?

If we are in ministry for any of these wrong reasons, Satan already has a foothold in us with which to work.

5. Do I want to sit and be served or am I here to serve?

6. Am I in the ministry to fulfill certain needs in me?

    - A need for acceptance?
    - A need for attention?
    - A need for a sense of self-worth, value or significance?

7. Am I in the ministry for personal financial gain?

    The Bible speaks a lot about the love of money being the root of all kinds of evil. It also warns leaders not to be greedy for gain. I must ask myself...

    - Am I a hireling?
    - Can I be bought?
    - Do I treat rich people differently than poor people?
    - Do I make merchandise of the people of God?
    - Do I see people as a means to meet my personal desires and goals?

8. Am I in the ministry for what I can get out of it personally?

Paul spoke of those who preached from strife, envy and personal ambition (Phil. 1:15-17).

Some indeed preach Christ even from envy and strife, and some also from goodwill: the former preach Christ from selfish ambition, not sincerely, supposing to add affliction to my chains but the latter out of love, knowing that I am appointed for the defense of the gospel. –NKJV

It's true that some are preaching out of jealousy and rivalry. But others preach about Christ with pure motives. They preach because they love me, for they know I have been appointed to defend the Good News. Those others do not have pure motives as they preach about Christ. They preach with selfish ambition, not sincerely, intending to make my chains more painful to me. – NLT

Paul also spoke of those who served their own belly or their own interests (Rom. 16:18).

For those who are such do not serve our Lord Jesus Christ, but their own belly, and by smooth words and flattering speech deceive the hearts of the simple. – NKJV

Such people are not serving Christ our Lord; they are serving their own personal interests. By smooth talk and glowing words they deceive innocent people. –NLT

In addition, Paul spoke of those who served to please men (Gal. 1:10,).

Obviously, I'm not trying to be a people pleaser! No, I am trying to please God. If I were still trying

to please people, I would not be Christ's servant.
– NLT

All of these questions that we ask ourselves, require raw honesty. All of us would like to believe certain things about ourselves. We would like to believe we are noble, we are humble, we are other's orientated, we only want the will of God and we only want to live lives that being glory and honor to the name of the Lord. Most of the time this is not completely true.

Purity in our desires is a struggle and it is not a battle that is won once and for all in this life. We need God's help. We need to realize that we need God's help. We need to stand with David and ask the Holy Spirit to assist us in searching our own hearts and help us to see where we need repentance and change (Ps. 139:23-24).

Maintaining a Servant's Heart

Examining our own heart is so important if we are to live as Christ lived, if we are love as Christ loved and if we are to serve as Christ served. As we examine our hearts compared to the heart of Jesus we soon realize that we need a spiritual heart transplant. This means putting Jesus on the throne of our lives and the center of our hearts. Leaders must maintain and continually cultivate the heart of a servant.

Jesus was very clear about those that would serve as leaders to His people. They had to be those that positioned themselves as servants who were willing to lay their lives down for others. In other words, all ministers are first and foremost the servants of the servants of the Lord. The New Testament makes this clear in referring to leaders in servant language such as:

- Servants of God (2 Cor. 3:6; 1 Th. 3:2).
- Servants of Christ (Rom. 1:1; 1 Cor. 4:1).
- Servants of the Gospel (Col. 1:23).

- Servants of the New Covenant (2 Cor. 3:6).
- Servants of the people of God (1 Cor. 3:5; 9:19).

Most leaders start out with this understanding of ministry, but if we do not guard our hearts, it is easy to lose that perspective. There are a number of things that will cause us to lose a servant's heart. It is easy to lose a servant's heart. It is easy...

- ❖ When people murmur and complain even after you have given yourself sacrificially to them.
- ❖ When you begin to believe that you have paid your dues, you have sacrificed enough and now you owe it to yourself.
- ❖ When you are hurt by those who you are trying to help.
- ❖ When you focus on the material success of others who are serving their own interests...and seem to be getting away with it.
- ❖ When you start listening to the humanistic lie that the best thing you can do for others is to do what is good for you.

Paul, the apostle, realized that all of our ministry life is an offering to God and that our mission is to serve others by lifting them up and releasing them into their place of function. With that understanding it was easy for him to die to himself daily, take up the towel and wash the feet of those given into his hands.

For though I am free from all men, I have made myself a servant to all... 1 Corinthians 9:19a

Exalting the Word of God

A big part of keeping ourselves pure is placing a high priority on the Word of God in our lives and in our ministries. In other words, we place the word of God above prophecies, books, podcasts and articles written by famous Christian men and women that we have grown to respect highly. It does not matter who says something or writes something, if what they are saying does not line up with the Word of God, the Word of God must always prevail.

With respect to the Word of God, this means

- Loving it!
- Preaching it!
- Teaching it!
- Meditating on it!
- Searching it!
- Practicing it!
- Being a lover of truth!

Many people are vulnerable to false doctrine because they have never really studied the Bible. They teach what they have heard other people teach. If they do not have solid principles of biblical interpretation, they can easily mishandle to the Word.

This means that we must choose the solid rock of the Word of God over miracles, dreams, visions, prophecies and other supernatural displays. The more you handle the true, the easier it is to identify the false...even in your own heart.

Sticking to the Basics

One of the best ways to avoid pitfalls in ministry areas is to never tire of the basics of Christianity. One of my mentors, Dick Iverson, used to tell us, "Keep the basic beautiful." New Testament Christianity is pretty simple. The basics of Christianity are still the keys to success. They will work in every generation. We must trust the basics.

This includes focusing on the ABC's or the fundamentals of Christianity including repentance, faith, water baptism, Holy Spirit baptism and discipleship. Jesus indicated that part of our commission is to teach all nations to observe all that He had commanded.

Often times, people are prone to deception and false teaching because they lack an understanding of the basic doctrines of the Bible. What does the Bible say about God, Man, Sin, Satan, Angels, Christ, Redemption, the Holy Spirit, and the Church? They say that the best way to teach people to identify counterfeit money is to have them handle the real so much that as soon as something doesn't feel right, red flags go up.

The basics also include building strong marriages and families. Some have said that the church is only as strong as the families are strong. If we breakdown in the home, we are vulnerable to attacks of the enemy.

Guarding the Flock

One of the primary functions of spiritual leadership is that of a watchmen. A watchman is someone who is on guard, watching for anything that could come in and cause damage to the work of God and the people of God. Paul told the Ephesian elders in Acts 20:28-31,

> *Therefore take heed to yourselves and to all the flock, among which the Holy Spirit has made you overseers, to shepherd the church of God which He purchased with His own blood. For I know this, that after my departure savage wolves will come in among you, not sparing the flock. Also from among yourselves men will rise up, speaking perverse things, to draw away the disciples after themselves. Therefore watch, and remember that for three years I did not cease to warn everyone night and day with tears.*

If we are going to be effective watchmen, we must be willing to test ministries that are making an impact on our sheep. This means that we cannot be intimidated by the signs and wonders that we see. This means that at times we need to be a little skeptical of the new and exotic (Pro. 15:15). It also means that we must be fruit inspectors (Mt. 7:16). Having a big building, a TV ministry or books in print does not authenticate a ministry.

As watchmen we must be willing to test doctrines and even judge prophecy. We must be willing to prove all things and hold fast to that which is good. In the next chapters of this book we will be taking more about evaluating winds of doctrine and discerning true and false doctrine or teaching.

In the appendix to this chapter I have given you some guidelines for judging prophecy. (**See Appendix**)

Maintaining First Love

Perhaps the most important thing for all of us to do, leaders included, is to work to maintain a first-love relationship with the Lord (Rev. 2:4-5). In other words, "Stay in love with Jesus." The closer we walk with Jesus in a daily life of submission and obedience the more we will be able to separate the true from the false (John 7:16-17, NLT).

> *So Jesus told them, "I'm not teaching my own ideas, but those of God who sent me. Anyone who wants to do the will of God will know whether my teaching is from God or is merely my own."*

Appendix, Judging Prophecy

Judging Prophecy

Prophecy is a precious gift of the Spirit that has been given to the church for the blessing of God's people. When it is functioning as God designed, it has a tremendous ability to bless, strengthen, encourage, motivate, inspire, lift, envision and challenge.

But, at the same time, prophecy that is abused or given in an unbiblical way can do serious damage, bring confusion and unrest, and misguide or mislead believing people who are sincerely looking for direction, divine counsel and a "word from God" for their life.

For this reason, Paul indicates in 1 Corinthians 14:29 that prophecy is to be judged. This is not real easy for us because we do understand that prophecy is a gift of the Spirit and because of the manner in which it is given. When a person gives a prophecy, it is usually given in the first person as if God is speaking (and indeed He is).

For this reason, it is easy for us to feel that if we judge this prophecy, we are in some way judging the Spirit of God. No one wants to put him or herself in such a position. And yet, God makes it clear that prophecy is not to be viewed as infallible. This means that it is not to be taken on the same level as the written word of God.

Prophecy comes through people who are fallible and can be affected by many different things that could have a bearing on a prophecy when given. For this reason godly people need to be discriminating as they listen to prophetic words and make a decision as to whether or not the prophecy is indeed from God in part or in full.

The Need for Judgment

Judging prophecy is very difficult for people to do, because it is difficult to judge the word without judging the person who is giving the word. No one wants to call another person into question or to seem to be argumentative. However, if prophecy is not judged, we do open ourselves up to being seriously misled in our walk with the Lord.

Christ was the only infallible ministry. Every person born into the world must contend with sinful tendencies that can flavor any action that they take. The Bible indicates that there will be false ministries. There will be false teachers, pastoral hirelings, false apostles and false prophets.

In addition, even valid ministries who have a good heart can "miss it" when it comes to giving counsel or uttering prophecy because it is so easy to get emotionally involved in situations and find oneself sharing one's own words or desires rather than a pure word from God. In addition, because God's people are at times so interested in "getting a word from God" that they exert pressure on prophetic ministries "to produce." This pressure can cause prophets to go "beyond the gift" to ensure that everyone gets a word.

Tests for the Prophetic

When testing prophecy there are several factors that should play into our judgment in the matter:

1. ### Test #1 – The Written Word of God

   The written Word of God is the ultimate criterion for judging prophecy (II Timothy 3:16). If the prophetic word is not in harmony with the Scripture it is to be rejected (Isaiah 8:19-20). Failure to do this can cause people to run the risk of placing prophecy on the same level as the Word of God. This will cause instability and will open the person up to being seriously misled.

2. **Test #2 – The Spirit or the Manner in which the Word is given.**

   The spirit in which the "word" is ministered can also be an indicator of its authenticity. While God has used the manner and mannerisms of prophets in unusual ways at times, the general rule is that prophecy will minister edification, exhortation and comfort (1 Corinthians 14:3) and lead to peace (1 Corinthians 14:33).

   The Holy Spirit may bring a rebuke, but most often it will be done in a pastoral way. Often when a word is harsh in its delivery it is because the person doing the prophesying is personally upset about something and is letting their own feelings, attitude or emotions about the matter enter into their message. Because of this, the "quickening" that they feel may or may not be brought on by the iniative of the Holy Spirit (Acts 21:4).

3. **Test #3 – The Conduct and Personal Life of the Prophet**

   God can certainly overrule the nature of the person prophesying and cause a true word to come forth from any vessel. If He can overrule the nature of a donkey, He can work through anyone. However, God's usual method of working is to speak through vessels who have set themselves aside in holiness and dedication to the Lord.

   When a prophet has a lifestyle that is ungodly, it brings the words that they speak into question (Jeremiah 23:15-16; 2 Peter 2:2). Ministries who have learned a life of daily obedience to God have also learned to hear the "still small voice" of the Spirit. Their words can be trusted more readily. The gifts of the Spirit must be motivated and impelled by the fruit of the Spirit. This will help ensure that the fruit of the prophecy is in line with the fruit of the Spirit.

4. **Test #4 – The Inner Witness of the Holy Spirit.**

   Since every true believer is inhabited by the Spirit of God and there is only one Holy Spirit, the Spirit of God within the believer should attest to the Spirit of God in the prophet (1 Corinthians 2:11-14).

   The inner peace of the Holy Spirit in this sense is a guiding force to help us discern whether or not this is a true word for us. God is not the author of confusion. If there is a lot of confusion in a person's spirit after the prophecy is given, the prophecy should be "put on the shelf" until peace returns (1 Cor. 14:33).

   The believer should be cautioned, however, not to take any prophecy lightly. They should spend specific time in prayer regarding its content and ask the Lord whether there might be any truth to it.

5. **Test #5 – The Confirmation of other Witnesses**

   If a word is to be established, it should be confirmed "in the mouth of two or three witnesses" (2 Corinthians 13:1). Even Jesus was willing to have his words examined in this way (John 5:31-47). These "witnesses" could include several things. One witness could be other prophetic ministries. Another witness could be pastors and other church leaders. Another witness could be parents and those that God has put over our lives. Even circumstances and other events in our lives that are almost like "divine coincidences" can bear witness to the authenticity of a prophetic word.

6. **Test #6 – The Edification by the Word Given**

   If a prophetic utterance is from the Lord, it should build up, admonish and encourage the people of God (1 Corinthians 14:3). If it does not accomplish this, it must be rejected. If the word is confusing, condemning, discouraging and brings a heaviness to an otherwise peaceful, uplifting setting, it is probably not from the Lord.

This is not to say that there is never a time or place for prophecy that is correctional in nature. But prophecy of this nature should be carefully screened by the leadership of the church and should still be ministered in a pastoral way so that the listener can more easily receive it.

7. **Test #7 – The Fulfillment of the Word Given**

If the prophetic word that is given is predictive in nature and it does not come to pass, the prophecy is not a true prophecy. This sounds so obvious, but it is amazing how people will try to "weasel out" of an inaccurate or presumptuous prophecy by accusing God of changing His mind, by blaming others for a lack of faith or prayer or by the claim that the Lord was only testing them.

The more a person brings forth inaccurate words, the more their prophecies will be considered suspect. Prophets whose words did not come to pass were not to be feared (Deuteronomy 18:20-22). In the Old Testament the erring prophet could actually be put to death. Today, we will most likely just ask them not to prophesy in the future.

8. **Test #8 – The Exaltation of Jesus**

If prophecy is to be proper in all of its aspects, it must ultimately exalt the Lord and bring glory to Him and Him alone (1 Peter 4:1). The result of prophecy is that people should see Jesus and be drawn to Him (1 Corinthians 14:25-25). Indeed John proclaims in the Book of Revelation that the "testimony of Jesus" is the spirit of prophecy (19:10), or as one translation says, "It is the truth concerning Jesus that inspires all prophecy" (Knox).

In the Old Testament even if the prophets words were true and came to pass, but the net result was that people were turned away from the Lord by their ministry, that prophet was to be considered false (Deuteronomy 13:1-5).

The caution here is that we must never let anything be the center of the prophetic experience but Jesus. We must not let our focus be on the individual through whom the prophecy comes, or on an institution, or on a method or style. All prophecy should inspire the worship of Jesus.

Who Judges the Prophetic?

There are various levels of judgment that should be operating in relation to prophecy. Each level of judgment should minimize the need for deeper levels of judgment. When everyone takes their God-given responsibility for the prophetic, we can grow in our confidence that prophecy will always edify and build up the people of God. One prophetic ministry gave this general guideline for all who prophesy, "We should be just as willing or eager to be judged as we are willing and eager to prophesy!"

1. Judgment Level #1 – The One Giving the Prophecy

The Bible clearly teaches that the "spirits of the prophets are subject to the prophets" (1 Corinthians 14:32). The Spirit of God does not overrule the will of man. When someone prophesies, they cannot say, "The Spirit made me do it." They cannot blame the Spirit of God for forcing them to prophesy in either an inopportune time or in an inappropriate manner. The Bible clearly teaches that we are responsible for what we say and do. Other translations of this same passage help us to understand more fully what is being said in this passage.

> *"Remember that a person who has a message from God has the power to stop himself and wait his turn"* (Living Bible).

> *"And the gift of prophecy does not take from the prophets the control of their own spirits"* (Conybeare).

In other words, people have total control of themselves when they give a prophetic utterance. It was the prophets who were associated with pagan temples that claimed they were overtaken by the gods and prophesied with an ecstatic frenzy. True prophets are to exercise control of their prophetic gift.

Paul said that if we would judge ourselves we would not be judged (1 Corinthians 11:31). While Paul was not speaking specifically about prophecy, self-analysis is clearly the first level of judgment that must take place in respect to any prophecy. This self-judgment should take place **before** the person who receives what they believe to be a word from God gives the prophecy.

The individual needs to render judgment on the content of his or her own word when measured against the word of God. Before they prophesy, they need to ask themselves some important questions.

- ✓ Is this word consistent with what the Bible says? Does it contradict the Scripture or violate any biblical principles?
- ✓ Will this word bring edification, exhortation or comfort?
- ✓ For whom is this word to be given? Is this a personal word for me or is it for the entire church?
- ✓ Am I a committed member of this church with a demonstrated love for and loyalty to the individual members of this congregation?
- ✓ Why do I want to give this word at this time? Is it in my heart to strengthen the church and its leadership?

- ✓ What is my personal attitude toward the congregation at this time? The pastor? The leadership?
- ✓ Is there any bitterness or lack of forgiveness in my spirit that might taint the word that is to be given?
- ✓ Is this word consistent with what God has been saying to the Church in this season? In this service?
- ✓ What seems to be the best time, place and context for this word to be given?

  Public setting? Private setting?
- ✓ What is the tone in which this word should be spoken?
- ✓ What is the manner in which the word is to be given? Orally to the pastor? Orally to the congregation? In writing to the pastor? Prophesied, exhorted or prayed?
- ✓ Is this the type of word that the pastor should be aware of **before** it is given to the congregation?
- ✓ Am I overstepping my authority in this congregation to give a word of this nature?
- ✓ Will this word put the pastor and leadership on the spot in front of the congregation? Am I painting myself or anyone else in a corner with this word?
- ✓ Am I using prophecy to bring a rebuke that I feel is needed, to speak my mind concerning the program or the vision of the church, or to get a major concern that I have off of my chest?
- ✓ Am I willing to allow this word of mine to be judged by others without feeling like everyone must agree with my personal analysis of it?
- ✓ Am I willing not to give this word if the leadership of the church feels that it is inappropriate?
- ✓ If this is a personal word for an individual, am I willing to request the presence of an appropriate person to listen to and judge this word?

- ✓ If my prophetic utterance proves to be inaccurate or does not come to pass, am I willing to take personal responsibility for it without blaming others for the result? Would I be willing to make a public statement acknowledging my error?

All of these questions will help the prophet minimize mistakes in the area of prophecy. But if this is to truly take place, a heartfelt desire for the serious evaluation of prophecy must be in the spirit of everyone who seeks to prophesy.

2. Judgment Level #2 – Other Prophetic Ministries

The New Testament seems to have prophets working together in tandem with either apostolic ministries or other prophetic ministries (Acts 13:1; 15:32). Paul indicates that in the context of prophetic ministry, the prophets should serve as a check and a balance to each other. "Let two or three prophets speak, and let the others judge" (1 Corinthians 14:29 NKJV).

There is no question that those who have been called by God to be prophetic voices to God's people have a special sensitivity to what God wants to say to His people. As prophetic ministries function together in the same setting, they should have a similar sensing of what God is trying to communicate to a person or to a congregation.

This is one reason why Paul undoubtedly encourages only two or three to speak, because in any given context they would all be receiving a similar message. How many times does a message have to be spoken before it is in effect delivered? The Bible answers this question also when it declares repeatedly that in the "mouth of two or three witnesses let every word be established" (2 Corinthians 13:1).

3. Judgment Level #3 – The Leadership of the Church

Ultimately, it is the responsibility of the leadership of the local church to render a judgment concerning any given prophecy. The Lead Pastor and the elders of the church have a God-given responsibility to feed, care for and protect the flock of God which is under their charge.

Paul makes this responsibility clear when he addresses the Ephesian elders in his meeting with them in Miletus (Acts 20:28-31). The elders were instructed to be overseers and watchmen, guarding against anything that would hurt or damage the people of God.

The Bible also instructs members of the congregation to submit to the elders of the church (1 Peter 5:5; Hebrews 13:17). The reason for this submission to the elders is that ultimately God holds elders accountable for what takes place in the congregation under their charge. We make the task of the elders easier when we recognize their authority and receive whatever correction they may want to give us with a good spirit.

The Need for and Value of the Prophetic

With so much being said about judging prophecy, it makes one wonder whether or not we should just "scrap" the idea of having prophetic ministry. Maybe it would just be easier to eliminate it altogether.

God forbid that we should ever think this way! We could say the same thing about raising children, building a home, cultivating friendships and even getting married. Just because something carries with it some challenges, it is no reason to do away with it. The problems associated with prophecy should never cause us to get to a place where we "despise prophecies" (1 Thessalonians 5:20).

The fact is that the blessing of the prophetic ministry so far outweighs any negative aspects of prophecy that eliminating this great gift from the church cannot even be considered. Churches that have no prophetic vision are missing a wonderful element of the whole Christian experience. Rather than seeking to eliminate the prophetic because of a few potential problems, we must seek how to harness this ministry for the ultimate purpose of strengthening the church of Jesus Christ.

Pastoring the Prophetic Ministry

If the experience of the church in the area of prophecy is to be a positive one, the Lead Pastor and the leadership team of the church must take an active role in leading and guiding the prophetic. Here are some guidelines that the leadership can follow into this important area.

1. **Teach people about prophecy.**

    Don't just wait for wrong behavior in this area to manifest itself and then try to correct it. This kind of training can promote a negative image for prophetic ministry. Teach the positive side of the ministry. Teach the people *before* there are problems so that they have truth to draw upon as they seek to operate in this ministry. Provide a positive environment for the emerging prophets to be discipled. Samuel did this in his "schools of the prophets" and he raised up a whole new order of ministry in Old Testament times.

2. **Teach people how to judge prophecy.**

    Put the tools in their hands that they need to have to evaluate their own prophecies and the prophecies of others. They will need this because at times they will be at other meetings or in other settings where prophecy is being given. They may have others who want to prophesy over them when you or someone from your leadership team is not present. If you have instructed them, they will have what they need to make their own judgments.

3. **Prophesy yourself.**

   People need models as they grow and develop in the things of the Lord. Teaching is important, but it must be accompanied by modeling. Pastors should stir up their own gift in this area and encourage all of their leadership team to do the same. This will give the people a positive example to follow.

4. **Don't allow strangers to prophesy** (as a general rule).

   There are many roving would-be prophets who are not committed to any one body of believers and who are not accountable to anyone for the words that they give. It should be clear in your assembly that there is no place for this kind of prophetic ministry. If someone that you do not know anything about comes to your assembly with a word, have them write it out and give it to you so you can pray over it with the other leaders, but do not have them speak it publicly. If your people are well trained, they will not listen to them anyway (John 10:4-5). There may be exceptions to this, but they should be rare.

5. **Provide a way for prophecy to be judged *before* it is given.**

   It is so much easier on everyone if prophecy is judged before it is given. Perhaps a microphone could be set up for this purpose and a member of the leadership team could assist people at the site. In this way the content of the prophecy could be shared with a church leader, and the leader could decide whether or not it should be given. A microphone can be very helpful so that people can hear more accurately what is being said and for the purpose of getting the prophecy on tape.

6. **Honor prophecy when it is given.**

   Once you have laid a good foundation for prophecy in your church, you should not only encourage it but you should honor it. We honor prophecy by giving it a place in our corporate gatherings and by taking it seriously when it is given. We also honor it when we make references to it in a service or when we integrate it into the life stream of the church in an immediate or ongoing way.

7. **Give people alternative outlets for prophecy.**

   Not everyone will be able to prophesy in a given service or public gathering. Leaders can encourage people come to them privately with what they feel the Lord is saying to them. People can also be encouraged to write down their prophetic insights and give them to a leader in the church. The leadership can discuss words of this nature and appropriate action can be taken when needed.

8. **Caution your people about prophetic abuses.**

   Prophetic zealots who will want to give them a personal word will approach many of your people. Encourage your people to seek appropriate witnesses for such words before they make any life adjustments on the basis of them. The wisdom acquired through many negative experiences needs to be exercised here so that people do not make rash decisions.

9. **Don't be afraid to judge prophecy.**

   While no one enjoys this aspect of pastoral ministry, we must be willing to make judgments at times especially where we feel that the church might be hurt if we do not make a judgment. Sometimes the action that we take may be done privately with the person who has prophesied "out of order." Other times, especially when some kind of response has been dictated by the prophecy, the issue may have to be handled publicly. The basic rule is to administer correction in the most gracious way possible while still getting the point across.

Conclusions

Prophecy is a great gift to the Church. We are instructed to not despise prophecies (I Thessalonians 5:20). In fact, we are to earnestly desire to prophesy (1 Corinthians 14:1). When we prophesy within the framework provided to us by the Word of God, prophecy edifies or builds up the church (1 Corinthians 14:4). If the church is going to be what God has called it to be, it will not get there without prophets and prophecy being fully released.

Part II

Discerning Doctrinal Trends

Chapter 6
Defining "Current Trends"

In this chapter I am transitioning from looking at true and false ministries to looking at true and false doctrines or teachings that can easily infiltrate the church world. This has been a problem since the inception of the Church in the First Century A.D. Paul had to deal with many false teaching whether he was dealing with a misapplication or Jewish law of the Old Covenant to the New Covenant in the Church Age or the blending of Christianity with secular philosophy.

The other apostolic writers also had to deal with the synergistic tendencies of the First Century to blend Christianity with other "ism" of the day. One of the most prominent of these was the blending of the tenets of Christianity with Gnosticism. Both Peter and John dealt with some of these abuses in the letters that they wrote to the churches of their day.

Paul warned in Ephesians 4 that the church could easily be blown about by every new wind of doctrine that might come their way (4:14). If you have lived any length of time in the Christian world, you know that we go through seasons where a new wave of doctrinal emphasis seems to periodically land on the beach. Much of what occurs has a very positive element to it. But there is also the tendency for it to come with some mixture. This is true because these teachings come through imperfect vessels.

These waves on the beach might be called "current trends" in the Body of Christ.

What are Current Trends?

In order to talk about current trends, we need to define our concepts from the beginning. The word "trend" means "an inclination in a particular direction, a general direction or a bent toward something." Some to the synonyms in our culture for this word include the following:

- Fashion
- Drift
- Direction
- Tendency
- Leaning
- Inclination
- Propensity
- Proclivity
- Impulse

Trends can be applied to almost any area of life. The reason why this is true is because all of life is in a constant state of change. Change is, in fact, one of the marks of something that is alive. Plato said as early as 399 B.C., "The seen is changing, the unseen is the unchanging." Paul said it this way in 2 Corinthians 4:18 (NIV),

> *So we fix our eyes not on what is seen, but on what is unseen. For what is seen is temporary, but what is unseen is eternal.*

In other words, we might say that the only things that is constant is change. Every aspect of our world seems to be subject to constant change including the world of nature, the world of science, the world of technology, the world of fashion, and the world of politics. You name it, everything is in a constant state of flux.

Trends also affect the world of the Church. If the church is indeed a "living organism" it automatically changes. One of the signs of life is change. Change happens for at least five reasons in the life of any church.

1. Change happens because of natural growth and the maturing process.
2. Change happens because of a progressive walk with the Lord.
3. Change happens because of improvements (from glory to glory).
4. Change happens because the church must adapt to a changing world.
5. Change happens because God is always pushing the church forward.

In this chapter we are looking at "current" trends. We know that there have been many past trends from which we can learn a great deal. But what do we mean when we say "current trends?" The word "current" is a relative term that means "recent, prevailing or present."

For the purpose of our study, we will be focusing on trends of the last 50 years. We will discuss some earlier trends to learn from history and see how some of the current trends might be nothing more than a recycling of previous cycles or trends. However, our immediate focus will be on the more present trends and forces that are shaping the church today.

We will be looking at trends as they pertain to the church world. We will not be looking at secular trends, although these are often intertwined. We will not be looking at trends in a particular local church, but we will focus on those movements that have touched the entire church world.

Positive Aspects of Trends in the Church

Often God uses trends or spiritual emphases in the present church world because of something that He is trying to accomplish in and through the Church in the current stage of God's unfolding purpose. God is very much involved in the building of the Church through the person of the Holy Spirit. The Holy Spirit has been a key player in the life of the Church from the very beginning.

Some trends reflect an emphasis that God is highlighting in a certain season. God understands the world-wide demands of each generation and knows what the church needs to move into at any given time to meet its unique challenge.

Some trends represent the restoration of a truth that has been lost to the church. The history of the church demonstrates that by the 3rd Century, the church had seemingly lost much of the dynamics of the Early Church as represented in the Book of Acts. The Church seems to have gotten to the place by the 14th Century that Luther's revelation of the "just shall live by faith" was a novel concept.

From Luther on, God has been restoring His church back to her former glory. Restoring such things as water baptism by immersion, holiness, healing, the baptism of the Holy Spirit, the gifts of the Spirit, and many other truths that seemed to have been lost in the experience of most of the church world. This work by God will continue until the Church is the beautiful expression of Christ to the world that God intended for it to be.

Some trends are aimed at refreshing the Church with a fresh breath of air from the Spirit of God. Peter preached in Acts 3:19 and referred to "times of refreshing" coming from the Presence of the Lord. It seems that there are times in God's economy where He feels the need to blow a fresh breathe of Holy Spirit air on the Church to enliven some to the bones that have grown weary or dry. Wuest in his New

Testament translation refers to these times as "seasons of revival."

Some trends are the result of adjusting methods to meet the unique demands of a generation or culture. In this case, we are not so much talking about doctrinal trends, we are referring more about the way we do things and how the church has to adapt its forms and methods to meet the current status of things in the culture of its world. It is always important to be able to separate what is commanded from what is only preferred. Methods change, biblical principles and doctrine should remain the same.

Different Trend Categories

Trends that circulate in the church world can fall into a number of categories. Some of the trends that we will reference are **doctrinal** in nature. These doctrinal trends might include such things as:

- Faith
- Prosperity
- Deliverance/Demonology
- Spiritual Warfare
- Dominion Theology
- Grace
- Etc.

Some of the trends that we will reference deal with **church structure**. These structural trends might include such things as:

- Discipleship/Shepherding
- Church Government
- Apostles and Prophets
- Church Groupings
- The Cell Church
- Etc.

Some of the trends that we will reference deal with **church methodology**. These methodological trends might include such things as:

- Church Growth Movement
- Church Marketing
- Seeker-Sensitive
- User Friendly
- Felt Needs
- Simple Church
- Etc.

Challenges of Examining Current Trends

Examining and evaluating current trends can be a challenge because of the tension produced by the pressures of the church staying relevant. This expresses itself in several ways.

1. Leaders must balance the tension between biblical conviction or principle and method, style, application or experience.

2. Leaders must balance the pressure to be culturally relevant, yet at the same time maintain a pure Gospel and promote a genuinely biblical experience.

3. Leaders must balance the desire to be open and sensitive to what the Spirit might be saying without being careless and gullible to the point of believing everything and being blown about by every wind of doctrine.

4. Leaders must balance the ability to be flexible, adjustable and innovative without compromising the timeless, universal and eternal.

5. Leaders must balance the challenge of being discerning, cautious and wise without overreacting and becoming critical, closed and judgmental.

6. Leaders must balance the ability to incorporate the truth contained in a current trend without losing perspective relative to the other truths of the Scripture.

We will be coming back to these dilemmas in the later chapters, but for now it is easy to see why we need to be in tune with the Holy Spirit and the wisdom that comes down from on high if we are going to navigate the winds.

Two Primary Premises

There are two primary premises about "change" that will serve as a basis for our further study of current trends. These premises will guide us as we go forward.

Premise 1 – *We are living in a world of change and, therefore, we must have an ability to adapt to that change if we are going to touch the present generation for God.*

A.W. Tozer (1897-1963) said, "The immutability of God appears in its most perfect beauty when viewed against the mutability of man. In God no change is possible; in man change is impossible to escape. Neither the man is fixed nor his world, and he and it are in constant change."

Alfred Whitehead commented on the church in a 1927 journal, *Science and the Modern World* saying, "Religion will not regain its old power until it can face change in the same spirit as does science. Its principles may be eternal, but the expression of those principles require continual development."

Abraham Lincoln (1809-1865) stated, "The dogmas of the quiet past are inadequate to the stormy present. The occasion is piled high with difficulty, and we must rise to the occasion. As our case is new, so we must think anew and act anew."

This premise has two parts. The first part of this premise acknowledges that we are living in the world of change. In our day, it takes less and less time for the world to become different. We could cite all kinds of statistics to support this but I will just highlight two. The top ten jobs in America listed in 2010 did not exist in 2004. Also, the amount of technical information is doubling every two years. As a result half of what students study in university in technical fields will be outdated by their third year of study.

The second part of this premise is that the church must have the ability to adapt to that change. The church is an adaptable institution that will function well in every time zone, political setting and culture of the world. The challenge for the leaders of the church is to be adaptable to world changes without compromising the Gospel or the clearly revealed principles of the Bible.

Premise 2 – *The Church has always been characterized by change that is related to the context or environment in which it finds itself.*

This premise acknowledges the fact that the Church was built by God to reach all people from every generation, every nation under every circumstance. If the context of the church is persecution, tolerance or freedom, the church can adapt its forms. If the context of the church is Eastern, Western or Developing World, the church can adapt its forms to become all things to all men. If the context of the church is the 1st Century or the 21st Century, the church has the power to be relevant, prophetic and to meet the needs of the world in which it exists.

In an effort to be relevant, it helps to know what the "essence" of the church is and what the luxuries are. What is that which is universal and what is only preferential?

As we move forward through this study we will refer back to these premises.

Chapter 7
The Challenge of Relevancy

The Church has always faced a unique challenge by virtue of the fact that it is designed by God to be an everlasting institution. Most institutions built by human beings have a lifespan. That is, they are only relevant for a season and, as things change, they become less and less relevant until they fade from the scene altogether. In the 1800's and early 1900's you may have had a thriving horse drawn buggy business. But when motorized vehicles became popular that business eventually lost its relevancy to society.

The Church on the other hand was meant to endure right up to the return of Jesus Christ. This brings us to our second premise discussed in the previous chapter. *The Church has always been characterized by change that is related to the context or environment in which it finds itself.*

This change has to do with understanding the current context of the church and being able to adapt to that context without destroying or diminishing the Gospel message and the mission of the Church.

In the world of today there are things happening in the world around us that can have a bearing on how the Church expresses itself. While this will vary a great deal from country to country, there are many trends that affect a large segment of society that have a direct bearing on the Church.

Current Societal Trends

While all of these current trends are not as significant in every nation of the world, because of the global nature of the modern world community, there is a gradual infiltration of these forces in all but the most primitive of cultures.

1. Changing definitions of the family

Because of the gay rights movement and the acceptance of alternative lifestyles, because of the astronomical rise in the divorce rate, because of the number of people choosing to co-habit without marriage, because of the number of single parent homes, the definition of the family is changing from God's definition of the family promoted in the Bible.

2. Changing definition of male and female roles

Because of the women's liberation movements which have produced an increase of abortion on demand, high percentages of women in the work force, the rise of day care for children and high levels of gender sensitivity there has been a change in the roles of men and women from that which is promoted in the Bible. In today's world it is ludicrous to speak of wives submitting to husbands.

Some of this has been caused by the absentee or renegade father who has not handled the spiritual leadership of his home well.

3. Changing in fields of science and medicine

Changes in these fields have created many ethical issues that did not exist in biblical times. Things like genetic engineering, artificial insemination, cloning, ultrasound, transplants, and cosmetic surgery (to name a few) has brought new challenges to church leaders.

4. **Changing technological advances**

   Changes in technology, computer science, telecommunications and the rise of The Internet have turned the world into a global community where any form of information is able to be accessed or transmitted quickly in a wide variety of ways. It is predicted that in less than five years you will be able to buy a relatively cheap computer that will have the capacity to store the entire accumulation of human knowledge.

5. **Changing in social structures**

   Changes in society have made it possible for people to live in complete isolation from others. If they want food they can order in. If they want entertainment they can access games, movies and a wide variety of things without ever leaving their bedroom. If they are looking for a friend or community they can log on to a "chat room." A person in South Africa can play chess with someone in Greenland if they so desire. People can even find their spouse without ever actually dating (A 2017 study suggests that 37% of heterosexual couples met online). Purchasing online has become a popular alternate to fighting your way through malls and traffic to the point that many retail chains have closed their doors.

6. **Changing in centers of influence and power**

   The centers of population, powers and influence are changing. There is a gradual shift from the United States and the European communities to the Pacific Rim nations including China, India, Japan, Korea and Indonesia. Soon China will have more English speakers than any other nation in the world.

7. **Changing in government involvement**

   Governments are getting more and more involved in things that will have an impact on the Church. Whether it be controlling the churches through taxation and audits or enacting laws that challenge the basic teaching of the Bible (anti-spanking, hate speech laws, etc.).

The church needs to be aware of what is going on around it so that it can adapt in order to present the Gospel to the world of today. We want to be like the men of Isachaar who understood the times and knew how to respond correctly to those times (1 Chr. 12:32a).

...of the sons of Issachar who had understanding of the times, to know what Israel ought to do...

All these men understood the temper of the times and knew the best course for Israel to take. –NLT

...men who knew the needs of the time and what exactly Israel ought to do. –Mof

The Church and Relevancy

As the Church finds itself in the cultural context of this day, it faces the challenge of being relevant. Even though the Bible was written thousands of years ago to a specific people with specific cultures, we must be able to extract that which is timeless and bring it into our time in a way that it can be received by in our culture and in our time zone.

The word "relevant" means "fitting or suiting given requirements." Some of the synonyms for this word include: applicable or pertinent.

"Since the church has been commissioned by Christ to extend His Kingdom throughout the earth, we are continually in need of evaluating our progress. Part of this evaluation has to focus on the world we are trying to reach. Do we understand where people are? Are we aware of the forces shaping their lives? Are we hindering our mission by being out of date? Are we preaching to kinds of people that do not exist anymore? Are we aiming our influence at a society that has moved out of our sights? Or, have we in our attempts to be relevant, compromised some of the very distinctives we should be confronting the world with?" –Ken Malmin

Today's church must be relevant to people and to society. When a church is relevant the people are better equipped to take their Christianity to the streets because the message of the church addresses the real issues that people face.

Attempts at Relevancy

In an attempt to be relevant to our culture today there are many churches that are trying various things. Most of these have come out of the church growth movement from the last forty years.

There is the ***"seeker-sensitive"*** movement. This movement seeks to make church services more "relevant" or at least more palatable and entertaining to people who are used to receiving information through multi-media. It attempts to rid itself of religious language and terminology (sometimes known as "Christianese") for the sake of those who are not familiar with Christianity.

Some of the characteristics of such churches would include the following:

1. More subdued worship
2. Virtual elimination of anything that might offend (e.g. tongues, prophecy, dancing, etc.)
3. Shorter services and preaching
4. Adults-only services
5. Contemporary music (perhaps even some secular)
6. Modern instruments
7. Fast moving presentations

8. Minimize anything confrontational (Altar calls, lifting hands, standing too much, etc.).
9. Allowing visitors space without embarrassment

There is the *"felt-need"* movement. This movement seeks to analyze where people are at and what their needs are and then structure its programs and ministries with those particular needs in mind. This is sometimes referred to as the "audience driven" approach.

Some of the characteristic of such churches would include the following:

1. Victim and abuse support groups
2. Focus on inner healing
3. Non-confrontation messages
4. Many homogeneous groupings

There is the *"technology"* movement. The term "movement" may not be the best word for this but it does represent a growing segment of the church. This movement employs modern technology and marketing strategies to grow the church. They utilize concepts that have proven effective in the business world and apply them to the various ministries and programs of the church.

Some of the characteristic of such churches would include the following:

1. Telemarketing strategies
2. Multi-media blitzes
3. User-friendly concepts
4. Target audiences
5. Multiple sites and simulcasting
6. Advertising (flyer campaigns, billboards, etc.)

7. Production arts (lighting, smoke machines, styling, etc.)

These are a few examples of people trying to reach the society in which they live by using the latest tools at their disposal. More movements could be listed, but these help us to get the basic idea that most local churches are constantly trying to figure out how to stay relevant in a rapidly changing world to the point that they may even attempt to do everything online.

The Primary Tension of Relevancy

When considering the of relevancy there seems to be a natural tension that can develop because the Church of Jesus Christ has a long history and is in some ways connected to all of those believers that have gone before us and the basic tenets of our faith is draw from writings that were produced some 2000 to 4000 years ago.

As a result, the issue of relevancy has a *positive* and a *negative* side. On the positive side, relevancy means that the church must be willing to change its forms and programs to face the demands of the culture in which it finds itself.

1. This means utilizing modern technologies to fulfill the great commission. All of the current technologies can be tremendous tools for the spread of the Gospel and the fulfillment of the great commission.

2. This means taking advantage of management techniques which are in essence an extension of the biblical principles of stewardship to become more efficient in what we do with the resources that we have.

3. This means addressing the issues that are truly facing the people to whom we minister to help them become ambassadors in their day to their generation.

4. This means being willing to evaluate our styles and methods of doing things to be sure that we are not needlessly offensive to the very people that we are trying to reach (Rom. 14:1; 15:1-2; I Cor. 9:22). Paul wrote in 1 Corinthians 9:20-22,

> *For though I am free from all men, I have made myself a servant to all, that I might win the more; and to the Jews I became as a Jew, that I might win Jews; to those who are under the law, as under the law, that I might win those who are under the law; to those who are without law, as without law (not being without law toward God, but under law toward Christ), that I might win those who are without law; to the weak I became as weak, that I might win the weak. I have become all things to all men, that I might by all means save some.*

On the negative side, relevancy must never be exalted above truth and can never lead us to compromise the eternal principles of God's Word to which all men must adapt themselves.

1. This means that while modern technologies should be utilized, they must not be abused and become a substitute for personal pastoral ministry. Our ability to produce special light shows and a cloud of smoke must never replace an actual living encounter with the presence of the Lord.

2. This means that while we employ managerial methods that will help us to be better stewards of our resources, we must not reduce the church to the level of a human business institution without reliance on the supernatural and the need for faith.

3. This means that while the church and its leaders must be in touch with the needs of the people and concerned about meeting those needs, they must not forget their central

need for a personal relationship with God and the purpose for which all healing is to take place, and that is to become a disciplined army of God, advancing with the sword of the Spirit to reclaim territory lost to the devil (the church is an army, not a comfort station, a boot camp not a summer camp).

4. This means that while the church should not be living in the Dark Ages in its "look" and approach to society, lines must be drawn when the Bible clearly addresses issues of morality, separation from worldliness, and our position in this world as strangers and pilgrims.

This challenge for church leaders is real. We do not want to become so irrelevant that we cannot reach the current generation for Christ, but we do not want to become so acceptable to the current generation that we miss the whole point of our existence in the first place. Every leader needs to ask for God's wisdom and the help of the Holy Spirit to find that balance for the sake of the harvest.

Chapter 8
The Challenge of Balance

Most of the difficult areas in life relating to discernment do not necessarily have to do with deciding between right and wrong. It often has to do with discerning between the good, the better or the best. It often has to do with discerning between how much emphasis should be placed on one thing as opposed to another.

The Importance of Balance

Some people react to the word "balance" because they feel that too much emphasis on it means that we never try new things or never really go anywhere. They see it as a word that inspires being overly cautious to the point where everything new is bad and the old is always better.

The truth is that we could never walk unless we were willing to be out of balance a good portions of the time. Walking involves a shifting of one's weight from balance to out of balance and back to balance again. When walking it is important to always come back to a place of balance or we risk tripping up or falling. That is something that is never to be desired.

Balance is important when it comes to the success of the church. The truth is, balance is important in every area of life. God is a God of balance. All of God's creation speaks of balance. The human body is perhaps the best demonstration of this. Balance is important for functional success in nearly every realm. If something or someone gets out of balance it is easy for them to stumble and fall.

There are many areas of life where balance is important. We need balance in our natural diet. This involves the right combination of protein, fat and carbohydrates. Too much or too little of any of these can result in physical problems. In addition, we need all of the essential vitamins and minerals that our body demands. Too much or too little of any of these can result in physical problems as well.

We need balance in our personal lives. Our schedules of work, exercise, rest need to be in proper proportion if we are to live a long and productive life. We need balance in our family lives. This means allowing the right time for ourselves, our families, our spouse and our church or ministry involvements. All of these areas are important and any one of them can get out of balance to the point where we start experiencing problems. The same is true of our social lives and the cultivation of friendships.

Balance is especially important in the life of the church. There are several aspect of this as it pertains to how a church functions. For our purposes here, I will highlight three main areas where balance is needed. We often need to find that narrow way that leads to life.

1. We need balance in our church life.

- Congregational ministry/Personal ministry
- Corporate activity/Individual activity
- Inreach/Outreach
- Preaching/Teaching
- Worship/Word
- Freedom/Order

2. We need balance regarding doctrine.

    - Divine Sovereignty/Human Responsibility
    - Law/Grace
    - Faith/Works
    - Gifts of the Spirit/Fruit of the Spirit
    - Extreme Authority/Anarchy

3. We need balance regarding church emphases.

    Many churches were built on or have become characterized by an emphasis. That is, the church is identified or known by a certain doctrinal belief or system.

    Some common emphases include the following:

    - Evangelism
    - Healing/Deliverance
    - Faith/Prosperity
    - Water Baptism (Baptists)
    - Baptism of the Holy Spirit (Pentecostals)
    - Prayer
    - Missions
    - Holiness
    - Prophecy/Dreams/Visions
    - Love/Forgiveness/Acceptance
    - Praise and Worship
    - Spiritual Warfare
    - Dominion
    - Family
    - Community
    - Grace

    Virtually any aspect of the church can become an emphasis. Sometimes the emphasis is reflected in the actual name of the church.

Balance verses Relevancy

When it comes to the issue of relevancy and church life there are some serious challenges that every church leader must face. These challenges can be summarize in seven areas.

1. INFLUENCE

Where does faith cease to influence culture and the culture begin to influence the church and its faith (John 17:6-19)? In other words, who is following whom?

Os Guinness in his book, *Dining with the Devil*, states, "Compared to the past, faith today influences culture less. Compared to the past culture today influences faith more" (pg. 16).

While the church often lags behind culture, the church is to be a prophetic voice to the culture. We are to be "the head and not the tail" (Deut. 28:44). We are to change the world; the world is not supposed to change us (Acts 17:6).

Some recent polls (at least in America) seem to indicate that what people profess to believe no longer makes much difference as to how they behave.

2. BECOMING ALL THINGS

Where does "becoming all things" to culture end and the church's responsibility to provoke people to "become all things" in Christ begin (Eph. 4:15; 2 Cor. 12:19)? Paul said this in Ephesians 4:14-15,

> ...that we should no longer be children, tossed to and fro and carried about with every wind of doctrine, by the trickery of men, in the cunning craftiness of deceitful plotting, but, speaking the truth in love, may grow up in all things into Him who is the head—Christ...

The New Living Translation renders verse 15 this way,

> *Instead, we will hold to the truth in love, becoming more and more in every way like Christ, who is the head of his body, the church.* –NLT

Is it right for us to be satisfied with leading people to less than the full expression of Christ in them? Is it right for us to try too hard to make people comfortable when they have many sin issues to deal with that are keeping them from fulfilling their destiny? What kind of Christians are we satisfied with in a day when the church is challenged to touch the world?

Os Guinness states that this modern focus "simultaneously makes evangelism easier—more people at more times in their life are more open to the Gospel—yet makes discipleship harder, because practicing the lordship of Christ runs counter to the fragmentation and specialization of modern life" (pg. 18).

3. NATURAL ABILITIES

Where does utilizing our natural abilities and strengths (arm of the flesh) begin to supplant or become an acceptable substitute for true visitation and revival (arm of the Spirit)?

Paul was clear that he did not want people's faith to rest on human wisdom when he wrote in 1 Corinthians 2:1-5,

> *And I, brethren, when I came to you, did not come with excellence of speech or of wisdom declaring to you the testimony of God. 2 For I determined not to know anything among you except Jesus Christ and Him crucified. 3 I was with you in weakness, in fear, and in much trembling. 4 And my speech and my preaching were not with persuasive words of human wisdom, but in demonstration of the Spirit and of power, 5 that*

your faith should not be in the wisdom of men but in the power of God.

Os Guinness states that this modern focus "undercuts true dependence on God's sovereign awakening by fostering the notion that we can effect revival by human means" (pg. 20).

The danger here is that we can become so clever in all of our techniques that we almost eliminate our need for God. Once we take our need for God and dependency on God out of the mix, "God experiences" soon give way to external conformity. When this happens, we lose the power to transmit our faith to the next generation. Our faith has become a formula instead of an experience with God.

Sometimes our success can actually undermine our succession!

> *But God forbid that I should boast except in the cross of our Lord Jesus Christ, by whom the world has been crucified to me, and I to the world.*
> Galatians 6:14

4. COMFORTABLE EXPERIENCE

Where does our attempt to make people comfortable leave off and our need to challenge our people to become living sacrifices and spend themselves and their resources on Christ and His kingdom begin? One pastor said it this way, "My job is to comfort the afflicted and afflict the comfortable." Paul said this in Romans 12:1-2,

> *I beseech you therefore, brethren, by the mercies of God, that you present your bodies a living sacrifice, holy, acceptable to God, which is your reasonable service. And do not be conformed to this world, but be transformed by the renewing of your mind, that you may prove what is that good and acceptable and perfect will of God.*

Jesus set a pretty high bar for his followers to get over if they were to be His disciples (Mt. 16:24-6; Luke 9:57-62).

> *Then Jesus said to His disciples, "If anyone desires to come after Me, let him deny himself, and take up his cross, and follow Me. For whoever desires to save his life will lose it, but whoever loses his life for My sake will find it. For what profit is it to a man if he gains the whole world, and loses his own soul? Or what will a man give in exchange for his soul?"* Matthew 16:24-26

Os Guinness states that "far from leading to an exodus, modern church growth often uses the ideology and tools of Egypt to make the people more comfortable in captivity" (pg. 21).

Where exactly does "the cross" come in (Gal. 2:20; 5:11, 24; 1 Cor. 1:23-24)? Do we really preach the "cross?" Can we really say that we knew nothing among you but Christ and Him crucified (1 Cor. 2:2)? When was the last time we preached on "mortifying the flesh" (Rom. 8:13)?

> *And those who are Christ's have crucified the flesh with its passions and desires.* Galatians 5:24

5. METHODOLOGY/THEOLOGY

Where do techniques, style and methodology replace or minimize truth and theology (1 Tim. 3:15)?

A famous Christian pollster and prolific author in the area of church growth confessed, "I don't deal with theology. I am simply a methodologist."

This is fine, but if we are not careful the result of this approach can be a "methodology" only occasionally in search of a "theology."

6. NUMERICAL GROWTH

Where does a desire for numerical growth compromise the necessity for spiritual growth as well?

If we focus too much on spiritual growth alone we can become exclusive, inward and almost cultish.

However, if we only focus on numerical growth we can come to the place where we have a lot of spiritual babies but no one that is coming to maturity (1 Cor. 3:1-3).

The early apostles seemed to be able to accomplish both (Acts 9:31).

> *Then the churches throughout all Judea, Galilee, and Samaria had peace and were edified. And walking in the fear of the Lord and in the comfort of the Holy Spirit, they were multiplied.*

They had both because they did not hide the truth. They told people what they needed to do without apology (Acts 2:37-40).

> *Now when they heard this, they were cut to the heart, and said to Peter and the rest of the apostles, "Men and brethren, what shall we do?" 38 Then Peter said to them, "Repent, and let every one of you be baptized in the name of Jesus Christ for the remission of sins; and you shall receive the gift of the Holy Spirit. 39 For the promise is to you and to your children, and to all who are afar off, as many as the Lord our God will call." 40 And with many other words he testified and exhorted them, saying, "Be saved from this perverse generation."*

7. HISTORICAL CONNECTION

Where does our desire for cultural relevancy end and our responsibility to those who have died in the faith begin (Pro. 22:28; 23:10; Jude 3)?

While we must have a voice to the present, we cannot totally extract or divorce ourselves from the church of the past. We must be careful that we do not forsake the "ancient landmarks" that are to be part of our modern heritage (Pro. 22:28; 23:10).

Many of the challenges faced by the church today, many of the philosophical and doctrinal journeys that the church takes are not unlike those of other generations. If we cannot learn from the mistakes or abuses of the past we are destined to repeat them.

If we cannot link ourselves back to the New Testament believers we will culturalize all of our theology in the name of relevancy and end up with no connection to "the faith once delivered" (Jude 3). Jude seems to think that this is something for which we must "contend."

> *Beloved, while I was very diligent to write to you concerning our common salvation, I found it necessary to write to you exhorting you to contend earnestly for the faith which was once for all delivered to the saints.*

When you read Paul's letters you get the distinct feeling that when he speaks of "the faith" he has in mind a body of truth that forms the basis of "our faith" (2 Cor. 13:5a).

*Examine yourselves as to whether you are in **the faith**.*

Notice also the following:

...obedience to the faith... Romans 1:5

...he that is weak in the faith... Romans 14:1

...stand fast in the faith... 1 Corinthians 16:13

...he now preaches the faith... Galatians 1:23

...till we all come to the unity of the faith... Ephesians 4:13

...if you indeed continue in the faith... Colossians 1:23

...rooted and built up in Him and established in the faith... Colossians 2:7

...holding the mystery of the faith with a pure conscience... 1 Timothy 3:9

...great boldness in the faith which is in Christ Jesus... 1 Timothy 3:13

...some will depart from the faith... 1 Timothy 4:1

...some have strayed from the faith... 1 Timothy 6:10

...rebuke them sharply, that they may be sound in the faith... Titus 1:13

O Timothy! Guard what was committed to your trust, avoiding the profane and idle babblings and contradictions of what is falsely called knowledge--by professing it some have strayed concerning the faith.
1 Timothy 6:20-21

Paul said that there were certain traditions that he had established that he wanted practiced in all of the churches (1 Cor. 4:17; 11:2).

Keys to Maintaining Balance

If balance can be achieved in all of the above areas, if Christians "were to use the best fruits of the managerial revolution constructively and critically, accompanied by a parallel reformation of truth and theology, the potential for the gospel would be incalculable" (Guiness, pg. 24).

So what are some of the ways to keep balance when introducing the change? Dick Iverson in his book *Maintaining Balance when Winds of Doctrine Blow* offers several keys (pages 57-88). Among his suggestions are these of which I will highlight only five.

1. Stick to clear scriptures to support your vision (2 Cor. 13:1).

   "The first principle to remember is that if a teaching is worth devoting your life to, and especially worth affecting the Christian community at large, then it is going to be stated repeatedly in the Bible!" (Iverson, pg. 59).

2. Major on the majors found in God's Word.

   "A church reduces its chances of going off on a tangent if it majors on what the Bible majors on and it minors on what the Bible minors on. We emphasize what God emphasizes! I am not suggesting that we are to ignore the minors, simply that we should not put a major emphasis on them" (Iverson, pp. 59-60).

3. Confer with other pastors (Pro. 11:14; 12:15; 15:22).

   Where there is no counsel, the people fall; but in the multitude of counselors there is safety.   Proverbs 11:14

   "Pastors need to relate to other pastors that they know and trust so that they can discuss and exchange ideas and trends that are stirring Christendom. Pursuing these kinds of relationships take time but they will ultimately help to safeguard the local pastor from possible imbalance" (Iverson, pg. 69).

4. Study it carefully (2 Tim. 2:15).

   "We in leadership who are commissioned to care for the flock of God must have the ability to see through all this glitter and emotional hype. We must not be gullible. We have to examine just exactly what is being said, and what the end result of this teaching is going to be" (Iverson, pg. 72).

5. Let others try it first.

   "To maintain a well-balanced church, be patient. When there is something going through the country, wait, be patient and let other churches try it first! Sometimes pastors may be a little reluctant to do this because they do not want to appear to be 'behind the times' in any way. Because of this it is easy for an insecure pastor to jump at everything that comes and as a result he becomes a spiritual 'guinea pig' that will test this new emphasis. For the sake of your people and long-term stability of your church, however, it is better to adopt a simple 'wait and see" attitude. That seems to be simple enough. But it may save you a lot of needless stress and many problems. Watch what is happening in the churches that are attempting to practice this truth and see how well they are doing. See if the implementation of that doctrine really works." (Iverson, pp. 77-78).

   Let me add another key of my own.

6. Develop clearly defined core values.

   An important process in the life of a leadership team is to develop biblical statements of your core values. Core values are truths that you will die for and cannot compromise. If you do not have any absolute lines that you will never cross it will be difficult to evaluate various trends that affect the church world.

For those who have never taken my *Vision and Values* course, I recommend it here. It takes you through the process of discovering, developing and articulating your vision and core values. It is available for free at www.churchleadershipresources.com. You will find it under School of Ministry and the course is 24 lessons on Vision and Values.

Chapter 9
The Challenge of Discerning the Winds

> *...that we should no longer be children, tossed to and fro and carried about with every **wind of doctrine**, by the trickery of men, in the cunning craftiness of deceitful plotting, but, speaking the truth in love, may grow up in all things into Him who is the head—Christ...*   Ephesians 4:14-15

The above passage speaks of winds of doctrine. When Paul wrote to the church at Ephesus, his concern was that believers grow up in their faith to the point that they were not vulnerable to every "wind of doctrine" especially those brought forth by "the trickery of men." The word "winds" in this context deserves a closer look.

The New International Reader's Version renders verse 14 as follows,

> *We will no longer be babies in the faith. We won't be like ships tossed around by the waves. We won't be blown here and there by every new teaching. We won't be blown around by the cleverness and tricks of people who try to hide their evil plans.*

Observations about Winds

Paul used the natural concept of the "wind" to talk about doctrines or teachings that blow through the Body of Christ.

For those of us who have been alive for any length of time, we have seen exactly what Paul is talking about. Sometimes these winds can have a positive effect, but at other times the effect can be more negative. With modern media, such winds of teaching are most likely more prevalent than Paul experienced in his day, because trends or winds of teaching can move rather quickly though the church world.

Winds are an apt symbol of doctrines that can circulate. In the natural sense, winds are caused by an unequal distribution of heat in the atmosphere. In other words, there has to be something out of balance or "unequal" to produce winds.

The direction from which a current comes determines its name. In other words, they are named based on their source not on their direction of travel. For instance, and East Wind is a wind that comes from the East. A West wind comes from the West.

In relation to winds of doctrine we can have good winds or bad winds based on the source from which they come. The question is, "Are these winds birthed in God and coming through people who are in tuned with the Holy Spirit? Or, are these winds inspired by Satan coming through the means of people with personal agendas or who are being used by evil forces to lead people away from the truth.

When two currents of air of different directions meet, a spiral motion sometimes results. This can result in turbulent winds, hurricanes or tornadoes that can end up being quite destructive.

Positive Purposes for Winds

In nature, wind can have a very positive effect. Even the Bible acknowledges that winds bring the clouds which bring the rains (1 Kgs. 18:44). Rains are essential for germinating the seed and ripening the harvest.

In Bible times, winds were also an aid to the farmer in winnowing the grain (Ps. 1:4; 35:5; Is. 17:13; 41:16). The farmers depended on the wind to help separate the wheat from the chaff in the winnowing process. In the winnowing process, the mature kernels of grain were heavy enough not to be blown about in the face of the wind, while the chaff (the outer husk) would be blown away. Psalm 1:4 says,

The ungodly are not so, but are like the chaff which the wind drives away.

In addition to winds helping the farmer, they also helped the seafarer. Winds were essential for ancient sea travel (Acts 28:13; Jam. 3:4). Without the winds, the only movement would have been with hard work and sweat. If the winds were favorable, the ship could ride the wind and take all of the work out of their voyage. However, if the winds were contrary, they would have serious struggle to the point where they may be hindered from reaching their destination.

Types of Wind in the Bible

The Book of Revelation makes reference to the four winds of the earth (Rev. 7:1). As you examine the Bible you will find four winds identified as the west wind, the south wind, the east wind and the north wind. It should be noted that each of these winds had their own characteristics. As we look at each of them, it should also be noted that all of these descriptions are seen in relation to the lands of the Bible. Their impact may be reversed for a different region or hemisphere.

First, we have the *west wind*. In Bible times, this wind was a cool wind that brought refreshing and showers. It was the most common kind of wind and the most desired. It was alluded to by Jesus in Luke 12:54:

Then He also said to the multitudes, "Whenever you see a cloud rising out of the west, immediately you say, 'A shower is coming'; and so it is."

Next, there was the *south wind*. This wind was warm and dry. It brought good weather unless it lasted too long, in which case, it brought scorching heat. This wind was also quite frequent. This wind was also referenced by Jesus in Luke 12:55-56:

And when you see the south wind blow, you say, 'There will be hot weather'; and there is. Hypocrites! You can discern the face of the sky and of the earth, but how is it you do not discern this time?

Next, there was the *north wind*. This wind was a strong, continuous wind that drove away the clouds and with them the rains. It was a disagreeable wind that often caused headaches and fever. There seems to be some confusion among the translators of Proverb 25:23 where it makes reference to the north wind. Some of the older translations render it as follows:

The north wind driveth away rain, as doth a sad countenance a backbiting tongue. –DRB

As the north wind holds back the rain, so an angry glance holds back slander. –NEB

Some of the more recent translations render it more like the New International Version.

Like a north wind that brings unexpected rain is a sly tongue—which provokes a horrified look. – NIV

So which is it? Does the north wind drive away the rain or does it bring the rain? The IVP Bible Background Commentary explains it this way. "In Israel a north wind does not bring rain but fair weather. It is therefore suggested that this proverb had its origin in Egypt where the north wind does bring the rain off the Mediterranean (five to ten inches per year in the delta)." So we could say, the north wind can either bring rain from off or the Mediterranean Sea if you are in

Egypt, but he north wind is a dry wind if you are in Palestine where the wind comes off of more arid lands.

Finally, there was the *east wind*. This wind was a scorning wind from the desert that was hot, gusty and laden with sand and dust. It occurred most frequently in May and October. It caused high temperatures quickly; it caused vegetation to wither; and it was often very destructive. The good news is that it seldom lasted for more than three days at a time. In Jeremiah this is called "the wind of the wilderness" (Jer. 13:24; See also Jer. 4:1; Hos. 13:15).

> *Therefore I will scatter them like stubble that passes away by the wind of the wilderness.* Jeremiah 13:24

In the dream of Pharaoh that was interpreted by Joseph the land of Egypt would be "blighted" by these east winds (Gen. 41:6).

> *After them, seven other heads of grain sprouted-thin and scorched by the east wind.* –NIV

> *Then suddenly, seven more heads appeared on the stalk, but these were shriveled and withered by the east wind.* –NLT

In was this wind that destroyed the house of Job and all of his children (Job 1:19, NLT).

> *Suddenly, a powerful wind swept in from the desert and hit the house on all sides. The house collapsed, and all your children are dead. I am the only one who escaped to tell you.*

In the realm of navigation on the sea, these winds were the most feared (Ps. 48:7; Acts 27:14).

> *Fear took hold of them there, and pain, as of a woman in birth pangs, as when You break the ships of Tarshish with an east wind.* Psalm 48:6-7

All of these winds can be brought on by the Lord for the fulfillment of His purpose (Ps. 78:26).

He caused an east wind to blow in the heavens; and by His power He brought in the south wind.

Wind Used Symbolically of the Holy Spirit

Most of the time when the Bible makes reference to "winds," it is speaking in a very literal and natural sense. But on some occasions, it may use the concept of winds in a more symbolic sense. There are two primary ways that the wind is used symbolically in the Bible. The first is in reference to the Holy Spirit of God and the second is in regard to doctrines or teachings that circulate through the world of the Church.

The Bible uses several symbols to illustrate the work and ministry of the Holy Spirit. The Holy Spirit is likened to fire (Mt. 3:11), to a dove (Mt. 3:16; Luke3:21-22; John 1:32), to oil or anointing (Luke 4:18; Acts 10:38; 1 John 2:20), to water (John 7:38-39; Is. 44:3) and to wind or breath (John 3:3-8; Acts 2:2; Is. 40:7).

In the Greek language, the word for spirit, wind and breath are the same. You determine how to render it based on the context in which it is used. The Holy Spirit is the wind of God or the breath of God. The Holy Spirit moves like the wind in at least five different ways.

1. The Spirit moves in a spiritual or non-visible realm (John 3:8, 1 Cor. 2:14).

   The wind blows where it wishes, and you hear the sound of it, but cannot tell where it comes from and where it goes. So is everyone who is born of the Spirit. John 3:8

2. The Spirit moves and operates at the Lord's command (Gal. 4:6; 1 Pet. 1:12).

3. The Spirit purges and cleanses the earth (Job. 37:21).

4. The Spirit moves as He wills (John 3:8; 1 Cor. 12:11).

5. The Spirit guides and impels the church (Acts 9:31; 13:4).

Winds Used Symbolically of Doctrine or Teachings

In addition to the wind being used symbolically to refer to the Holy Spirit, winds are also used to describe doctrines or teachings that circulate through the church world. We have cited Paul's word from Ephesians 4:14-15 before, but this is how it reads from the Berkeley Version.

As a result, we should no longer be babes, swung back and forth and carried around with every changing whiff of teaching that sprints from human cunning and ingenuity for devising error; but, lovingly attached to truth, we should grow up in every way toward Him who is the Head—Christ.

When these winds of doctrine are in balance and in harmony with the truth of the Scriptures, they can be refreshing and they are necessary for movement in the church. However, it they come to us out of sync with the Scriptures or they come in a way that is extreme and imbalanced, they can be destructive and damaging to the local church and the people that are in the church.

James makes reference to double minded people who can be like a wave of the sea driven and tossed by the wind (Jam.1:6). The word "tossed" that he used in this passage means "agitated or tossed first from one side and then from another." Unfortunately, that is the state of many believers who are feeding on truth and error at the same time.

Positive and the Potential Negative Effects of Winds?

There are three main types of flow described in the Bible—wind, water and rain. All of these can be positive or negative forces depending upon intensity, source and how they are controlled.

	POSITIVE FLOWS	NATURAL / SPIRITUAL RESULTS	NEGATIVE FLOWS	NATURAL / SPIRITUAL RESULTS
W I N D	Winds Breezes Zephyr	Refreshing, Cooling Gentle moving Delicate touching	Gale Cyclone Tornado Blast	Violent Destructive Devastating Upheaval
W A T E R	Currents Rivers Streams Flow	Advancement Progression Movement Continuity	Whirlpool Eddy Flood Tsunami	Introversion Dizziness Loss of Direction Drowning
R A I N	Rain Showers	Enlivening Growth Harvest	Storm Hurricane Deluge	Commotion Turbulence Loss of harvest

As you can see from the above chart, there are common characteristics of positive flows. Some of the common, positive characteristic include forces that are in control as opposed to when they are out of control, forces that are channeled as opposed to when they are being wild and random, forces that are desirable because they bring blessing and benefit to mankind.

You can also see that the opposite is also true. There are common characteristics of negative flows. Some of these common, negative characteristics include forces that are out of control as opposed to being in control, forces that have no boundaries or guidelines that they follow and forces the lead away from blessing into destruction.

The water that is channeled is a river and can be guided and directed to the field where crops grow and give life. But that same water without banks to the river can become a flood.

God's Relationship to the Winds

When it comes to the wind, whether we are talking about natural winds or winds of the Spirit, God is in control. John got a revelation of angelic beings holding the four winds (Rev. 7:1).

After these things I saw four angels standing at the four corners of the earth, holding the four winds of the earth, that the wind should not blow on the earth, on the sea, or on any tree.

When Jesus came and walked among us, He demonstrated supremacy over the elements, stilling the storm (Mt. 8:26; Mark 4:37; Luke 8:23) and walking on the waves (Mt. 14:24, 32; Mark 6:48-51).

Now when He got into a boat, His disciples followed Him. 24 And suddenly a great tempest arose on the sea, so that the boat was covered with the waves. But He was asleep. 25 Then His disciples came to Him and awoke Him, saying, "Lord, save us! We are perishing!" 26 But He said to them, "Why are you fearful, O you of little faith?" Then He arose and rebuked the winds and the sea, and there was a great calm. 27 So the men marveled, saying, **"Who can this be, that even the winds and the sea obey Him?"** Mathew 8:23-27

God uses the winds to test us. The winds can test us in at least three ways, just like they can test a structure that is built by man. Jesus told the story of the two builders who built houses. Both houses experienced the winds and the rains. One house stood the other one did not.

Winds can serve as a test to approve that which is good. In 1 Corinthians 11:19, Paul wrote, "For there must also be factions among you, that those who are approved may be recognized among you." The Message Bible says it this way, "The best that can be said for it is that the testing process will bring truth into the open and confirm it."

Winds can also serve as a test to see if we truly love the truth. Notice what Paul says in 2 Thessalonians 2:9-12, (NLT):

> *This evil man will come to do the work of Satan with counterfeit power and signs and miracles. He will use every kind of wicked deception to fool those who are on their way to destruction because they refuse to believe the truth that would save them. So God will send great deception upon them, and they will believe all these lies. Then they will be condemned for not believing the truth and for enjoying the evil they do.*

Finally, winds can serve as a test to help us exercise and develop our spiritual senses. The writer to the Hebrews reminds us that "solid food belongs to those who are of full age, that is, those who by reason of use have their senses exercised to discern both good and evil" (Heb. 5:14).

16 Warning Signs of Potential Turbulence

Winds of doctrine are circulating continually in the church world. How do we discern a good wind from a bad wind or a strengthening wind from a destructive wind? There are some warning signs that should be in the back of the mind of every mature believer.

As believers we are instructed to watch or be watchful (Acts 20:31; Rom. 16:17; Phil. 3:2; 1 Th. 5:6; 1 Pet. 5:8; 2 Pet. 3:17-18). Peter wrote in 2 Peter 3:17-18 (NLT),

> *I am warning you ahead of time, dear friends, so that you can watch out and not be carried away by the errors of these wicked people. I don't want you to lose your own secure footing. But grow in the special favor and knowledge of our Lord and Savior Jesus Christ. To him be all glory and honor, both now and forevermore. Amen.*

Also in 1 Peter 5:8, he wrote (NLT),

> *Be careful! Watch out for attacks from the Devil, your great enemy. He prowls around like a roaring lion, looking for some victim to devour.*

Peter's instruction here is to "Watch out!" Here are sixteen things for which we should "watch out."

1. Watch out for the word "new" especially when associated with "revelation."

> *History merely repeats itself. It has all been done before. Nothing under the sun is truly new. What can you point to that is new? How do you know it didn't already exist long ago?*
>
> Ecclesiastes 1:9-10, NLT

Paul preached the whole counsel of God (Acts 20:27). He warned the Galatians about those who would add to the basic doctrine that he had taught (Gal. 1:6-10).

There is something about people in that they always want something that is "new." There is a feeling that new is better. In reality, the truth is the truth in every generation. I do believe it is important to keep the old fresh by the way we handle it and feed it to others. But the basics of Christianity are not going to change. They will safely navigate us to the return of Christ.

God's revelation to man is complete in the Word of God. The Spirit of God may bring new understanding or illumination concerning the revealed Word of God, but this new understanding cannot violate the proper, biblical principles of interpretation (See: *Interpreting the Scripture* course at my website:
www.churchleadershipresources.com

It must represent the word "rightly divided" (2 Tim. 2:15).

2. Watch out for anything that requires "private interpretation" (2 Pet. 1:20).

Paul wrote this in 2 Corinthians 11:1-4 (NLT):

> *I hope you will be patient with me as I keep on talking like a fool. Please bear with me. I am jealous for you with the jealousy of God himself. For I promised you as a pure bride to one husband, Christ. But I fear that somehow you will be led away from your pure and simple devotion to Christ, just as Eve was deceived by the serpent. You seem to believe whatever anyone tells you, even if they preach about a different Jesus than the one we preach, or a different Spirit than the one you received, or a different kind of gospel than the one you believed.*

People love to tell you about truths that they uncovered through deep prayer or study—or worse yet, from a vision, dream or angelic visitation. How many cults have originated by the appearance of an "angel of light?" (2 Cor. 11:14). The word of God is still the standard. God's path and plan are not complex and God has no delight in concealing Himself or His truth from His people.

> *Finally, my brethren, rejoice in the Lord. For me to write the same things to you is not tedious, but for you it is safe.* Philippians 3:1

The Gospel and the way to salvation is basically simple as opposed to complex. God has designed His plan for man in such a way that it is readily open to all who are born of the Spirit (2 Cor. 4:3). There are some ministries who are filled with pride who would seek you make their followers overly dependent upon them. In this way they can control them though their deeper understanding.

3. Watch out for those who major on the minors.

> *This will be the third time I am coming to you. "By the mouth of two or three witnesses every word shall be established."* 2 Corinthians 13:1

Whenever someone uses one or two obscure passages of Scripture to develop a whole system of thought, a red flag should go up.

Every major or essential truth is taught clearly and repeatedly in the Bible. It is important never to build a doctrine on one verse alone or on an unclear passage.

The Mormons justify the baptism for the dead from a verse in the New Testament (1 Cor. 15:29).

> *Otherwise, what will they do who are baptized for the dead, if the dead do not rise at all? Why then are they baptized for the dead?*

Although studying the context of this passage will shed great light on the subject, the fact that no other verse in the Bible suggests that this was the practice of the Early Church should be sufficient to throw up a red flag.

4. Watch out for extremes or truth out of balance.

> *Enter by the narrow gate; for wide is the gate and broad is the way that leads to destruction, and there are many who go in by it. Because narrow is the gate and difficult is the way which leads to life, and there are few who find it.* Matthew 7:13-14

Jesus spoke of the narrow way that leads to life. Often times the narrow way or the right path is the narrow line or the balance between two extremes.

A good example of this is the debate over Calvinism and Armenianism. In the extreme, both of these views are dangerous. The extreme Calvinist view that promotes the idea "once you are saved you are always saved" can lead to the abuse of grace. However, the extreme Armenian view that promotes the idea that you have to get saved again every time you fall into sin is also dangerous and breeds a terrible fear and sense of insecurity before a loving heavenly Father.

Each of these views use certain key verses to support their views. However, the truth is most likely some place in the middle. We are eternally secure upon obedience.

This is just one example, but there are many others:

- The concept of faith must be balanced by the concept of works (Jam. 2:18).

- The concept of the goodness of God must be balanced by the concept of the wrath of God (Rom. 11:22).

- The concept of mercy of God must be balanced by the concept of holiness and justice of God (Ps. 85:10).

- The concept of prosperity and blessing must be balanced by the concept of persecution and sacrifice (2 Tim. 3:12).

This does not mean that God will not lead pastors to emphasize a certain aspect of truth during a season in the life of a local church to bring biblical understanding, but it does mean that after the truth has been emphasized it will once again be integrated back into the body of truth in a balanced way.

5. **Watch out for anything that promises "instant maturity."**

Paul wrote in Philippians 3:12-16 (NLT):

> *I don't mean to say that I have already achieved these things or that I have already reached perfection. But I press on to possess that perfection for which Christ Jesus first possessed me. No, dear brothers and sisters, I have not achieved it, but I focus on this one thing: Forgetting the past and looking forward to what lies ahead, I press on to reach the end of the race and receive the heavenly prize for which God, through Christ Jesus, is calling us. Let all who are spiritually mature agree on these things. If you disagree on some point, I believe God will make it plain to you. But we must hold on to the progress we have already made.*

Maturity by its very definition implies a constant and a steady growth. Sanctification is a process that began when we were born again in Christ Jesus and it will continue right up to the return of the Lord.

> *...being confident of this very thing, that He who has begun a good work in you will complete it until the day of Jesus Christ...* Philippians 1:6

Many people are looking for an instant cure for all of their difficulties. If people are led to believe that they can solve their problems by casting out a demon, chanting a certain phase or "mantra," experiencing a particular type of prayer by a particular type of person, getting a prophetic word from the "man of God" or fasting certain foods, they will go through just about anything.

People can run for this remedy or that remedy and never find what they are looking for because there is no instant cure for their problem. They are going to have to come through the "eye of the needle" which involves repentance from sin, denying themselves, putting on the armor of

God, resisting the devil, fighting a good fight and following hard after the Lord.

In every case, they are going to have to do the work. The solution will not come from outside of them by someone doing something for them. Jesus has already done for them everything that needs to be done. Their solution will come from inside of them when they tap into the grace of God for themselves each and every day of their lives for the rest of their lives.

6. Watch out not to judge a truth primarily on the basis of external signs that may follow.

> *The coming of the lawless one is according to the working of Satan, with all power, signs, and lying wonders...* 2 Thessalonians 2:9

The miraculous signs that someone may perform do not verify or authenticate what the person is saying. Simon Magnus was a man who exhibited many signs and wonders and claimed that he was a messenger of God (Acts 8:9-11). When people saw the signs they tended to believe everything that he said.

Remember, we learned earlier in this book that in the last days there will be many false christs, false prophets and false apostles that will be able to function in the miraculous. The Bible speaks of "lying signs and wonder" that can lead us to accept or believe things that are not true (2 Th. 2:9).

Signs are to follow believers as they exercise the gifts of the Holy Spirit (Mark 16:15-20), but believers are not to be those who seek after or run after signs (Mt. 12:39). Too many believers see a person operating in the miraculous and assume that it authenticates them as a ministry and affirms their doctrine no matter how they line up with the Scripture.

7. Watch out for teachings that elevate emotional experiences above the principles of God's Word.

> *For we did not follow cunningly devised fables when we made known to you the power and coming of our Lord Jesus Christ, but were eyewitnesses of His majesty. 17 For He received from God the Father honor and glory when such a voice came to Him from the Excellent Glory: "This is My beloved Son, in whom I am well pleased." 18 And we heard this voice which came from heaven when we were with Him on the holy mountain. 19 And so we have the prophetic word confirmed, which you do well to heed as a light that shines in a dark place, until the day dawns and the morning star rises in your hearts; 20 knowing this first, that no prophecy of Scripture is of any private interpretation, 21 for prophecy never came by the will of man, but holy men of God spoke as they were moved by the Holy Spirit.*
>
> 2 Peter 1:16-21

At times people can exalt visions, dreams, personal prophetic words and displays of the miraculous above the simple word of God. Peter had some of the greatest experiences that any human being could have, but he was able to say we also have a prophetic word which is even "more sure" than this (KJV). He was of course referring to the Scripture.

We know that the last days will be characterized by lying signs and wonders (2 Th. 2:9). We know that false ministries can and will operate in signs and wonders (Mt. 24:3-5, 11, 24-26). We know that the ability to operate in the gifts of the Spirit does not authenticate the ministry but the ministry is authenticated by the fruit of the Spirit (Mt. 7:16, 20). So why are we so easily led by these things? Or why do we believe because we had an emotional encounter that it must prove what was being taught?

As Christians we must trust the Word of God above our own subjective experiences or we will get off balance.

8. Watch out for spiritual language used to justify carnal desires (1 Tim. 6:3-10; Jam. 4:1-4).

> *But as we have been approved by God to be entrusted with the gospel, even so we speak, not as pleasing men, but God who tests our hearts. For neither at any time did we use flattering words, as you know, nor a cloak for covetousness--God is witness.* 1 Thessalonians 2:4-5

This is a very subtle thing to watch out for. There are certain things that have always and will always appeal to the carnal man. Everyone can get excited about driving new cars and living in expensive homes, especially if your doing so it can be seen as a mark of spiritual maturity. If I can clothe my greed or covetousness in a cloak of spirituality and thereby justify it, this has great appeal to my "flesh man" or carnal nature.

People have justified all sorts of things from adultery to drunkenness in the guise of spirituality. Taking obscure verses out of context, refusing to balance them with other scriptures and twisting them to fit their questionable interpretation, they sin and they lead others into the same sins.

The "flesh man" rebels against the concepts of selflessness, sacrifice and laying down one's life. Words like "repentance, tribulation, affliction and suffering" are not things that people want to include in their spiritual vocabulary.

If there is a way to reason around the cross and a way to clothe our self-centeredness in spiritual sounding phrases then we can keep our carnal nature and make it our religion.

9. **Watch out for teaching that promotes health, wealth, success and happiness with no mention of cost, pain, persecution, and even personal loss.**

> *But what things were gain to me, these I have counted loss for Christ. 8 Yet indeed I also count all things loss for the excellence of the knowledge of Christ Jesus my Lord, for whom I have suffered the loss of all things, and count them as rubbish, that I may gain Christ 9 and be found in Him, not having my own righteousness, which is from the law, but that which is through faith in Christ, the righteousness which is from God by faith; 10 that I may know Him and the power of His resurrection, and the fellowship of His sufferings, being conformed to His death, 11 if, by any means, I may attain to the resurrection from the dead.*
> Philippians 3:7-11

> *Yes, and all who desire to live godly in Christ Jesus will suffer persecution.* 2 Timothy 3:12

The Bible teaches that the way to live is to die. The way to exaltation is humility. It teaches that all who live godly in Christ Jesus will suffer persecution (2 Tim. 3:12) and that we must all through much tribulation enter the kingdom of God.

Paul referred to his own journey this way in 2 Corinthians 6:4-10 (NLT):

> *In everything we do we try to show that we are true ministers of God. We patiently endure troubles and hardships and calamities of every kind. We have been beaten, been put in jail, faced angry mobs, worked to exhaustion, endured sleepless nights, and gone without food. We have proved ourselves by our purity, our understanding, our patience, our kindness, our sincere love, and the power of the Holy Spirit. We*

have faithfully preached the truth. God's power has been working in us. We have righteousness as our weapon, both to attack and to defend ourselves. We serve God whether people honor us or despise us, whether they slander us or praise us. We are honest, but they call us impostors. We are well known, but we are treated as unknown. We live close to death, but here we are, still alive. We have been beaten within an inch of our lives. Our hearts ache, but we always have joy. We are poor, but we give spiritual riches to others. We own nothing, and yet we have everything.

Perhaps Paul was not spiritual enough to avoid these things in his life. I kid. Many men and women of God have been tortured for their faith and yet were considered great in the eyes of the Lord (Heb. 11:32-39).

I am not suggesting that Christians are not to enjoy life and see many victories. I am only suggesting that whatever we do, we do it for His glory and not our own.

10. **Watch out for teachings that will not work in every culture as easily as they do in the most prosperous and least persecuted of cultures (Tit. 1:5).**

When Paul laid down some principles by which to live, they were truths that were relevant and applicable to all. He wrote to the believers in Corinth and let them know that his teaching was not just for them. He said, *"And so I ordain in all the churches"* (1 Cor. 7:17c).

God's truth cuts across all generations and all cultures. God's word is eternal. If we are properly interpreting the word of God, there is no place on earth where these principles will not work. There is only one Gospel. There is not one Gospel for America, another for China, another for Africa or another for the Moslem nations of the world.

If anything that I am teaching and preaching does not work equally as well in the Third World as it does in the First World, I need to re-examine what I am teaching. God's word is universal.

11. **Watch out for doctrines that sidestep confession, repentance, restitution and forsaking sin and release you from personal responsibility for your deeds.**

> *Therefore, King Agrippa, I was not disobedient to the heavenly vision, but declared first to those in Damascus and in Jerusalem, and throughout all the region of Judea, and then to the Gentiles, that they should repent, turn to God, and do works befitting repentance.* Acts 26:19-20

Confession, repentance, restitution and forsaking sin are still the foundation of the Christian's walk with the Lord. There are many today who are offering love, acceptance and forgiveness without the basis for truth established. True recovery can never take place without dealing with sin in a biblical manner.

12. **Watch out for doctrines that diminish the power of the cross and the work of repentance in your life (Gal. 1:6-10).**

> *For I determined not to know anything among you except Jesus Christ and Him crucified.*
> 1 Corinthians 2:2

There is a great deal of blending of psychology into Christian counseling today. Many would espouse the idea that the Bible is an old book that does not take into account many of the current scientific research regarding man's behavior patterns. They imply that the application of the Word of God alone to people's lives is insufficient to meet the needs of modern man. They may say that we need the Bible plus __(fill in the blank)__ .

There is a place for scientific study relative to man and how he functions, however, only the Bible has the ultimate answer to man's emotional and psychological needs.

13. Watch out for doctrines that are not willing to be questioned or tested.

Paul wrote to the believers in Thessalonica to "Test all things; hold fast what is good" (1 Th. 5:21). John reminded his followers "do not believe every spirit, but test the spirits to see whether they are from God (1 John 4:1). Paul commended the believers in Berea who were open to what he was teaching, but also searched the Scriptures thoroughly to verify them as God's truth.

These were more fair-minded than those in Thessalonica, in that they received the word with all readiness, and searched the Scriptures daily to find out whether these things were so. Acts 17:11

God's people need to be wary when they find spiritual leaders who react when their teaching is challenged or when they are asked for scriptures to substantiate what they are teaching. Truth does not have to be defended. It will always bear up under scrutiny.

The Berean believers were not deemed rebellious when they searched the Scriptures upon hearing a new teaching; they were called noble or fair-minded. One translation says that they were of a "nobler disposition" (WNT).

There are three ways to respond to any new teaching that we may hear. One is to reject it immediately because it is not part of our tradition. That is foolish and assumes that one has heard it all. Second is to believe what is being taught immediately without scrutiny. That is gullibility and can lead to all sorts of error.

The third one that is to be preferred is to be like the Bereans, openly listen, hear it out and then scrutinize it against the Scripture before you embrace it and integrate it into your body of truth and lifestyle.

14. Watch out for doctrines that lead to spiritual pride or exclusivity.

> *Then if anyone says to you, "Look, here is the Christ!" or "There!" do not believe it. For false christs and false prophets will rise and show great signs and wonders to deceive, if possible, even the elect. See, I have told you beforehand. Therefore if they say to you, "Look, He is in the desert!" do not go out; or "Look, He is in the inner rooms!" do not believe it.* Matthew 24:23-26

There will always be those who pattern themselves after the "Gnostics" of old who promote the idea that they have a secret body of knowledge that is reserved for those who are more spiritual and want to journey into the "deep things of God."

People are invited into this inner circle of people who often meet in homes and rarely have any local church leadership present. These teachers often set themselves up against the leadership of the local church and explain that "your pastors and leaders have not received this higher revelation."

There are teachers today who would divide the Body of Christ into select groupings or companies. All of this teaching is divisive and produces schisms in the church. Paul tells us very clearly that there is but "one body" (Eph. 4:4).

15. Watch out for teachings that promote individuals and a dependence on individuals above Christ.

> *John's disciples came to him and said, "Teacher, the man you met on the other side of the Jordan River, the one you said was the Messiah, is also baptizing people. And everybody is going over there instead of coming here to us." John replied, "God in heaven appoints each person's work. You yourselves know how plainly I told you that I am not the Messiah. I am here to prepare the way for him--that is all. The bride will go where the bridegroom is. A bridegroom's friend rejoices with him. I am the bridegroom's friend, and I am filled with joy at his success. He must become greater and greater, and I must become less and less. He has come from above and is greater than anyone else. I am of the earth, and my understanding is limited to the things of earth, but he has come from heaven. He tells what he has seen and heard, but how few believe what he tells them!*
> John 3:26-32, NLT

Jesus said that John the Baptist was the greatest prophet who ever lived (Luke 7:28) and yet no one had any greater spirit of humility. His sole mission was to point people to Jesus. When this was accomplished he felt he was a true success. When evaluating a message, ask yourself, "Whom does this elevate? Whom does this promote?"

The whole point of any ministry is to point people to Jesus, to assist them in becoming dependent on God alone and to guide them into an intimate relationship with the Holy Spirit.

16. Watch out when the vessel does not confirm the message.

Jesus was clear that ministries were not to be judged based on the gifts or anointing that they seem to possess but by the fruit that is manifest in their lives.

> *Beware of false prophets, who come to you in sheep's clothing, but inwardly they are ravenous wolves. You will know them by their fruits. Do men gather grapes from thornbushes or figs from thistles? Even so, every good tree bears good fruit, but a bad tree bears bad fruit. A good tree cannot bear bad fruit, nor can a bad tree bear good fruit. Every tree that does not bear good fruit is cut down and thrown into the fire. Therefore by their fruits you will know them.*
> Matthew 7:15-20

Believe it or not there are many who espouse a particular truth who live their lives in serious sin.

Ensuring Our Safety

With the potential for all of these negative winds and turbulence, how can we ensure that we will not be blown off course or deceived by these winds? One thing we can do is to pay attention to the 16 warning signs that I just pointed out. These are defensive measures. But we can also go on the offense against such deception by focusing on three key things.

First, we should continually cultivate our personal relationship with the Lord. Paul wrote this to the believers at Ephesus who were doing well up to that point (Eph. 1:15-23). This is what he told them:

> *Therefore I also, after I heard of your faith in the Lord Jesus and your love for all the saints, 16 do not cease to give thanks for you, making mention of you*

in my prayers: 17 that the God of our Lord Jesus Christ, the Father of glory, **may give to you the spirit of wisdom and revelation in the knowledge of Him, 18 the eyes of your understanding being enlightened; that you may know what is the hope of His calling, what are the riches of the glory of His inheritance in the saints, 19 and what is the exceeding greatness of His power toward us who believe, according to the working of His mighty power 20 which He worked in Christ when He raised Him from the dead** *and seated Him at His right hand in the heavenly places, 21 far above all principality and power and might and dominion, and every name that is named, not only in this age but also in that which is to come. 22 And He put all things under His feet, and gave Him to be head over all things to the church, 23 which is His body, the fullness of Him who fills all in all.*

Second, we should focus on becoming a lover of the truth. The more we love God and His Word, the more we give ourselves to the Word, the more we put the Word of God deep in our hearts and the more we live in the Word, the more we will be safe from deception. Paul wrote the following to the believers in Thessalonica (2 Th. 2:9-12):

The coming of the lawless one is according to the working of Satan, with all power, signs, and lying wonders, and with all unrighteous deception among those who perish, because **they did not receive the love of the truth**, *that they might be saved. And for this reason God will send them strong delusion, that they should believe the lie, that they all may be condemned who did not believe the truth but had pleasure in unrighteousness.*

Finally, we should focus on the practice of daily obedience to God's voice (John 7:17). Hearing God's word and doing it is still the sure foundation upon which every Christian's life is to be built. This is equated to building on a rock foundation that can weather the most severe winds and waves that might come against it (Luke 6:46-49). Jesus said the following to His followers (John 7:17):

> *If anyone wills to do His will, he shall know concerning the doctrine, whether it is from God or whether I speak on My own authority.*

Concluding Thoughts

In all these guidelines we want to remember that God uses winds to bring positive growth, change and movement.

Most of the winds have an element of truth and contain something that God is really wanting the church to hear. This is why it is critical to use righteous judgment to test the winds. I heard Jack Hayford say once that winds of doctrine that come through the church are like waves on the beach. When the tides are coming in the waves can bring a lot of good things to the shore. When they recede they can leave a lot of debris on the beach. We want to prove all things, hold fast to the good and spit out the bones (so to speak).

Chapter 10
Present Day Trends

There have been several significant movements since the middle of the Twentieth Century. There is plenty of room to question some of the emphases of each of these movements in terms of how they expressed themselves in practical terms, but there is no doubt that some significant things were being said in the midst of these movements.

In this chapter I would like to mention a few of the most recent trends or movements and talk about the positive contribution that each of them made.

The Charismatic Movement

During the Charismatic Movement that dominated the 1960's and early 70's there was a strong emphasis on the assimilation of many of the previously illuminated truths into many of the historic denominations. The Baptism of the Spirit, speaking with other tongues, and renewed worship forms were incorporated into many denominational groups. In addition many new "independent" churches were built on the principles of church government that were an emphasis of the 1948 visitation. In fact, the fastest growing churches in the world today are independent charismatic churches.

The Discipleship Movement

While this movement caused a lot of confusion, it also brought a focus on the importance of spiritual authority, the need for believers to go on to maturity and the development of strong Christian character. Its failure had to do primarily with methodology and the application of the truth. The word "shepherding" became a negative word and equated to "controlling" and abusive leadership. The fact that those leading this movement did not have a clear understanding of the importance of the local church also contributed to the problems that would ensue.

The Dominion Movement

This movement like so many others came with problems. I refer back to Jack Hayford's comment when he said moves of the Spirit are like the waves that break onto a beach. Each wave that comes in brings with it two things—it brings in life (the positive) and it brings in debris (the negative). The Dominion Movement was flawed in terms of its biblical hermeneutic. Many who preached this doctrine did so out of scripture passages that were taken out of context. It also went to such an extreme that it almost left one to believe that God's plan of evangelism had more to do with the "ballot box" than preaching of the Gospel.

What it did bring in more of a positive way was an understanding that the Church of Jesus Christ is not going to be defeated. In fact, the church is to be the head and not the tail. The church need not be intimidated by the world. The church has a mission to touch every aspect of society and be salt and light to the world. It emphasized that Christianity is not just something that is practiced on Sunday morning, but we are to take the principles of the Kingdom into every sphere of life including the marketplace. It emphasized that every believer extends the kingdom by bringing believers to Christ and promoting God's agenda in the earth (Gen. 1:26-28).

The Faith and Prosperity Movement

Like so many of the movements before, certain proponents of this movement tended to go to an extreme which led many to conclude that they were making merchandise of the Gospel. Phrases like "name it and claim it" or "if you can dream it you can receive it" became misguided mottos associated with these truths.

The truth is that God does want us to be people of faith (What is the alternative?—people of unbelief!). He wants us to step out at the word of the Lord and walk on water when Jesus beckons us. He does want to prosper his people. However, divine prosperity is not just about money. It is not about making us wealthy so that we can fulfill selfish desires. It is about fulfilling destiny and walking under the canopy of God's blessing. It is about having strong families, good friendships, whole bodies, sound minds and freedom from bondage. It is about accomplishing the mission.

10 Positive Contributions of these Movements

While other movements could easily be added to the above list depending on one's personal perspective on the last few years, these particular movements carried with them some vital aspects of truth.

1. Covenant Relationship

The emphasis here was on the fact that in the Body of Christ we are our brother's keeper and that we should endeavor to establish relationships that focus on accountability one to another.

2. Family Life

The emphasis here was on principles of raising godly families to establish foundations for many generations. Many ministries arose with a focus on family, marriage and child rearing. Along with this many local churches put a stronger emphasis on Youth and Children's Ministry.

3. Spiritual Authority and Government

The emphasis here was that the local church is a place of spiritual authority and that we cannot be fully covered spiritually unless we are properly connected and in right relationship to the authority that God has placed in our lives.

4. Christian Character

The emphasis here was on the fact that we need more than the gifts of the Spirit if we are to fulfill the mission of Christ. We need the character of Christ. Christ-likeness is still the goal of the individual believer.

5. Small Group Ministry

The emphasis here was on the two-fold approach to building the saints in the New Testament Church. There was the corporate gathering for the purpose of celebration and mission fulfillment and there was the smaller gathering for the purpose of evangelism and body ministry.

6. Apostles and Prophets

The emphasis here was on a releasing of these ministries in a way that truly builds the church. The functioning of these ministries in a biblical way is essential for the church to come to full completion. (I encourage you to get my book, *Apostles, The Fathering Servant*).

7. Men's Movement

The emphasis here was on restoring men to their first responsibility of being the priest in their homes. Groups like the Promise Keepers were used to help men not to see themselves primarily as providers but also as protectors, spiritual leaders and shapers of arrows for the Lord (Ps. 127:3-5).

8. Dominion and the Kingdom of God

The emphasis here was on the "greater commission" given to Adam to subdue the earth. This involves the church getting involved in the issues of life on earth. This involves the church being a prophetic voice in all areas of society including politics, science, business, the arts and education. In this regard we are not talking about church programs we are talking about people who belong to Christ becoming involved and bringing the influence of Christ to bear in all arenas of life.

9. City Reaching

The emphasis here was on believing for entire cities to be reached for the Lord. The model here is the city of Samaria that turned to the Lord under the ministry of Philip (Acts 8:4-8).

10. Pastor's Unity, Pastor's Conferences, Pastor's Prayer, City-wide Prayer

The emphasis here was on seeing the Body of Christ come together beginning with the spiritual leaders. During this season there has be a rise of pastors' and church leaders' conferences, pastors' prayer gatherings and city wide prayer. Most of these expressions cross denominational lines as God is bringing His people together.

"Now Words

There are some "now" words or current concepts that God seems to be emphasizing in this season. These are winds of the Spirit that God is blowing on the church to meet the demands of this season in the life and progress of the Church. All of these things are key biblical concepts and have been true for all time, but in this present hour there seems to be an urgency in God's economy to make these points of focus.

For the purposes of this study, I am only highlighting four of these concepts. I am sure that all of you could add others of your own. Some of the things that the Holy Spirit is saying are for us as individuals as we continue on our path of personal growth and development. Some of the things that we are hearing are prophetic words to our local church as we continue to become a more effective instrument in God's hands. But here I am highlighting a few things that seem to be more universal in the Body of Christ at large. These are the ones that will be my focus.

1. Prayer, Intercession, Spiritual Warfare

Prayer, of course, is something that is a part of every season of visitation. Revival usually begins when people separate themselves in prayer and fasting. We are presently in a season where many prayer movements are being birthed. They reflect a spiritual hunger in the people for God to move to a deeper more powerful level in God.

2. Evangelism, Discipleship, Harvest

As we get closer to the harvest at the end of the age, we can expect a greater emphasis on evangelism. The church growth movements of the last few years are reflective of this. Many books and plans of evangelism have been promoted in the last few years including God's Master Plan of Evangelism, Evangelism Explosion, Lifestyle Evangelism, Servant Evangelism, Spirit-Filled Evangelism, Etc. Along with that many missionary movements have seized the concept of finishing the commission and reaching the remaining unreached people groups of the world.

More recently much is being said Christ's commission to make true disciples of those who come to Christ. As we prepare for the return of the Lord, it is essential that believers become deeper and move from followers to true reproducing disciples. I encourage you to check out my three discipleship manuals designed to move people forward in their walk to destiny. *Next Steps 1.0* is subtitled Securing the Foundation, *Next Steps 2.0* is subtitled Moving to Maturity. *Next Steps 3.0* is subtitled Discovering My Purpose.

3. Church Planting

A significant voice in the world today is coming in the area of church planting. Many have realized that the harvest will only be retained as local churches are established to disciple, equip and release those who have come to the Lord. There seems to be a strong emphasis on church planting being the object of all missionary endeavors.

4. Signs and Wonders

Many who have seen the magnitude of the task at hand and the increasing population of the earth are contending for a greater release of the miraculous power of the Holy Spirit in the Church of today. Many are expecting the spirit and the power of Elijah to be upon the church in the last days. They see this as part of the supernatural equipment that man needs to be able to finish the commission that has been placed on the Church by God Himself.

While signs and wonders have been a part of every major movement in the last century, it is needed today in a greater and more general way. It is needed to fall upon the entire church not just a few individual superstars. As believers in our day deepen their relationship to the Holy Spirit and becoming true disciples, this should be the outcome.

Evaluating a Trend

The whole point of this book is to assist the believer in evaluating ministries, trends and winds of doctrine that circulate in the world of the church. The following are the type of questions that should be asked about any trend that arises in the church world:

1. Is this trend based on a clear biblical foundation?

2. What are the key verses substantiating this trend or doctrine?

3. Is the biblical interpretation of these verses based on solid hermeneutical footing?

4. Are there any scriptural principles or precepts that seem to be contrary to this trend?

5. Is this trend something that was taught by Jesus and the Apostles, practiced in the Book of Acts and explained in the Epistles?

6. Is there any historical evidence that something similar to this has taken place in the past? If so, what was the ultimate result? If not, why not?

7. Do those who preach this truth have a lifestyle that is consistent with the character of Jesus?

   - In love
   - In humility
   - In servant-like spirit
   - In the absence of greed
   - In the fruit of the Spirit

8. Do those who preach this truth point you toward or draw you away from your local church leadership?

9. Does this teaching reinforce the unity of the Church or does it tend to divide?

10. Will this teaching work in any culture in the world?

11. What is the fruit in the lives of people who experience this truth?

12. What is the long-term benefit of this truth to the local church?

My Prayer

My prayer for all who read this book is the same as the prayers of Paul the Apostle to the Ephesian Church.

Ephesians 1:15-23, NLT

Ever since I first heard of your strong faith in the Lord Jesus and your love for God's people everywhere, I have not stopped thanking God for you. I pray for you constantly, asking God, the glorious Father of our Lord Jesus Christ, to give you spiritual wisdom and insight so that you might grow in your knowledge of God.

I pray that your hearts will be flooded with light so that you can understand the confident hope He has given to those He called—His holy people who are His rich and glorious inheritance. I also pray that you will understand the incredible greatness of God's power for us who believe Him. This is the same mighty power that raised Christ from the dead and seated Him in the place of honor at God's right hand in the heavenly realms.

Ephesians 3:14-21, NLT

When I think of all this, I fall to my knees and pray to the Father, the Creator of everything in heaven and on earth. I pray that from His glorious, unlimited resources He will empower you with inner strength through His Spirit. Then Christ will make His home in your hearts as you trust in Him. Your roots will grow down into God's love and keep you strong. And may you have the power to understand, as all God's people should, how wide, how long, how high, and how deep His love is. May you experience the love of Christ, though it is too great to understand fully. Then you will be made complete with all the fullness of life and power that comes from God. Now all glory to God, who is able, through His mighty power at work within us, to accomplish infinitely more than we might ask or think. Glory to Him in the church and in Christ Jesus through all generations forever and ever! Amen.

More Books By Bill Scheidler

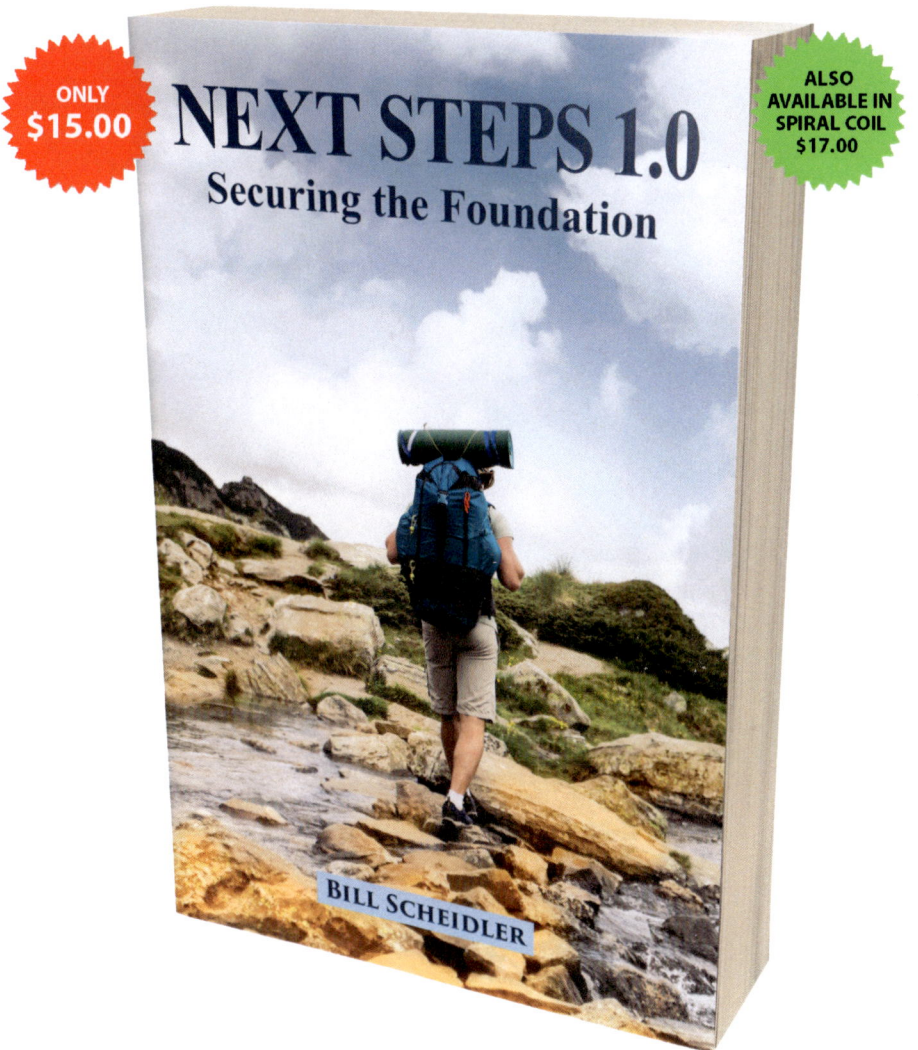

ONLY $15.00

ALSO AVAILABLE IN SPIRAL COIL $17.00

Next Steps 1.0 is the first in a series of three books all designed to bring the believer into a deeper relationship to God. The book focuses on ensuring that every believer's foundation is truly built upon the ROCK, Christ Jesus. Its purpose is to take the reader on a personal journey that involves inspecting their personal foundation in the faith with the view to ensuring that none of the basic building blocks to victorious Christian living are missing in their life and experience. It is meant to be a preparation step to the next book in the series, *Next Steps 2.0* which guides the believer onto the path toward greater maturity.

Order At: www.BTJohnsonPublishing.com
1-866-260-956 ● info@btjohnsonpublishing.com

More Books By Bill Scheidler

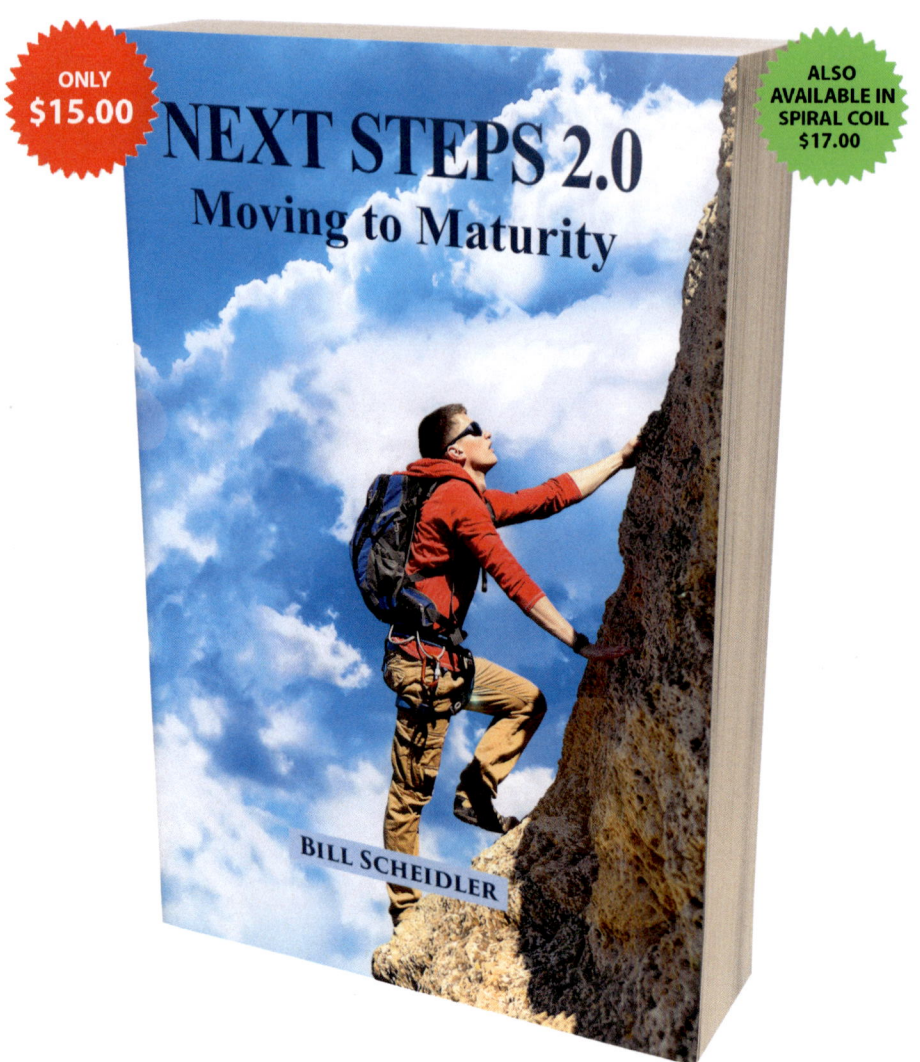

In *NEXT STEPS 1.0* the goal was to solidify our foundation as believers in Christ and to make sure that as we go forward our life is truly established on the ROCK. In *NEXT STEPS 2.0* our goal is to move on to maturity in our walk with Christ. The Bible teaches that the path of the just is a progressive one that is continually moving forward from level to level or from glory to glory. As you prayerfully study through *NEXT STEPS 2.0*, you will cultivate some to the disciplines of the Christian life that will help you to succeed as a Christian in your day to day life. It will also equip you to be *more effective in your witness of Christ and your testimony to those which do not yet have a relationship with Christ.*

Order At: www.BTJohnsonPublishing.com
1-866-260-956 ● info@btjohnsonpublishing.com

More Books By Bill Scheidler

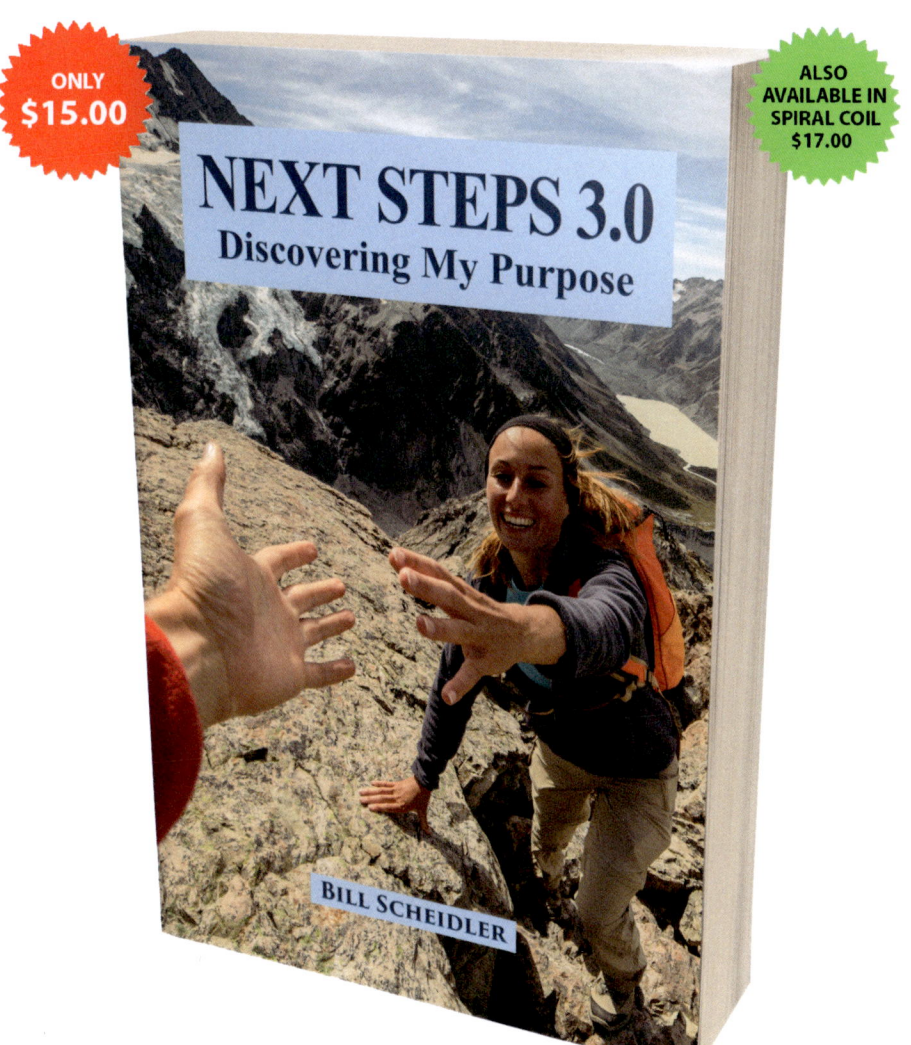

In Next Steps 2.0 the goal is for us to consistently move on to maturity in our walk with Christ. Here in *Next Steps 3.0*, our goal is to discover our life purpose and place of ministry that God has designed set for us in the Body of Christ. It is clear from the word of God that we are all fashioned by God with a purpose in mind. We have been given gifts, talents and abilities that are not just for ourselves, but they have been given to us so that our lives can be a blessing to others. God has a plan for our life that includes our being an instrument in God's hands to extend His kingdom here on earth and to align with His eternal purpose that was established from the foundation of the world. Working through this book will help you to discover your destiny.

Order At: www.BTJohnsonPublishing.com
1-866-260-956 ● info@btjohnsonpublishing.com

More Books By Bill Scheidler

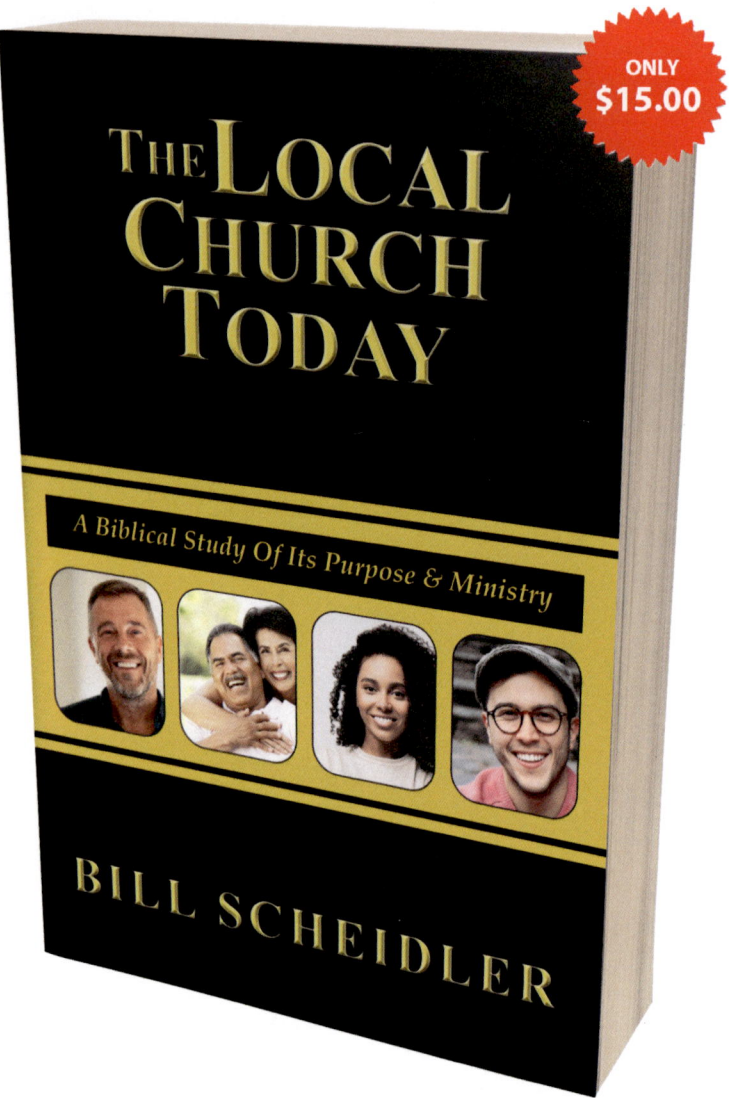

This book is intended to help you better understand what God's glorious purpose in the Church is, and what is your individual part in that purpose is...

It will give you fresh vision from God's perspective—rather than from man's. Your faith will be strengthened to see the Church of Jesus Christ fulfill all that God has purposed!

Order At: www.BTJohnsonPublishing.com
1-866-260-956 ● info@btjohnsonpublishing.com

More Books By Bill Scheidler

Every Pastor desires church growth. Methods come and go, constantly change, but principles have an eternal quality about them. These nineteen keys will provide excellent resource material. This wise book reflects many years of serious thought, hands-on experience and interaction with church leaders around the world. The author is actively involved in training leaders, writing and assisting the growth and development of churches both nationally and internationally.

Order At: www.BTJohnsonPublishing.com
1-866-260-956 n   info@btjohnsonpublishing.com

More Books By Bill Scheidler

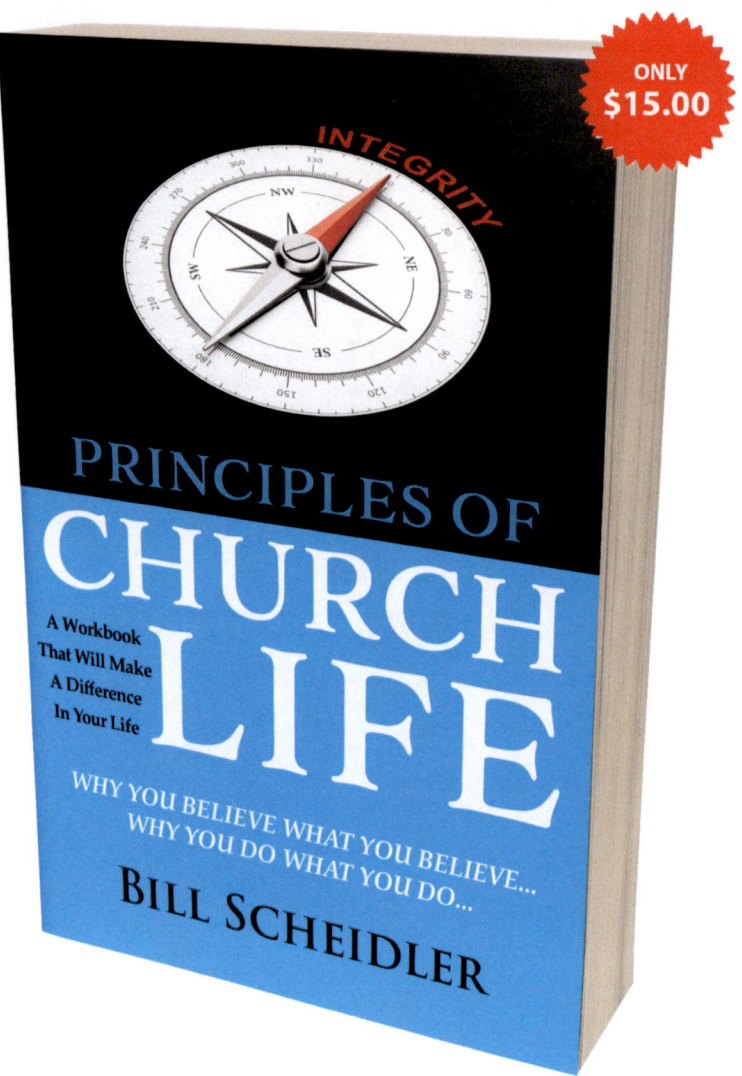

The book aims to provide the church membership with a solid foundation necessary for the maturing and growth of the people. Its goal is to bring new church members into a place of knowledge and understanding so they can, in faith, begin to contribute their part to the overall purposes of God.

With 25 lessons of clear, detailed and topical teachings, Principles of Church Life walks the believer through the importance of Church life and lays out God's dynamic plan for the Church and His desire for the committed active involvement of every member

Order At: www.BTJohnsonPublishing.com
1-866-260-956 ● info@btjohnsonpublishing.com